THE DOCTRINE OF THE ṢŪFĪS

BY THE SAME AUTHOR

Arabic Poetry (1965)
Fifty Poems of Ḥāfiẓ (1947)
Modern Arabic Poetry (1950)
(with P. Grech) *Dun Karm, Poet of Malta* (1961)
(ed.) *Religion in the Middle East* (1969)
(ed.) *Poems of al-Mutanabbi* (1967)
(ed.) *FitzGerald's 'Salaman and Absal'* (1956)

THE DOCTRINE OF THE ṢŪFĪS

(Kitāb al-Ta'arruf li-madhhab ahl al-taṣawwuf)

Translated from the Arabic of
Abū Bakr al-Kalābādhī
by
A. J. ARBERRY

Formerly Sir Thomas Adams Professor of Arabic in the University of Cambridge

The right of the University of Cambridge to print and sell all manner of books was granted by Henry VIII in 1534. The University has printed and published continuously since 1584.

CAMBRIDGE UNIVERSITY PRESS

CAMBRIDGE
NEW YORK PORT CHESTER
MELBOURNE SYDNEY

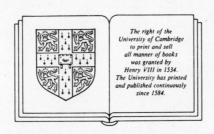

Published by the Press Syndicate of the University of Cambridge
The Pitt Building, Trumpington Street, Cambridge CB2 1RP
40 West 20th Street, New York, NY 10011-4211, USA
10 Stamford Road, Oakleigh, Victoria 3166, Australia

First published 1935
First paperback edition 1977
Reprinted 1978 1979 1989 1991

Printed in Great Britain by the
Athenaeum Press Ltd, Newcastle upon Tyne

Library of Congress Cataloguing in Publication Data

al-Kalābādhī, Muḥammed ibn Ibrāhīm, 10th cent.
The doctrine of the Sūfis = Kitāb al-ta'arruf
li-madhhab ahl al-taṣawwuf.
Reprint of the 1935 edn published by University
Press, Cambridge
Includes index.
1. Sufism — Early works to 1800. I. Arberry,
Arthur John, 1905-1969. II. Title
BP189.26.K3813 1977 297'.4 76—58075
ISBN 0 521 21647 8 hardback
ISBN 0 521 29218 2 paperback

CONTENTS

Introduction

Some years ago my friend and teacher, Professor Nicholson, was so generous as to put at my disposal his manuscript of the Arabic original of the work the English translation of which is now presented to the public: the *Kitāb al-Ta'arruf li-madhhab ahl al-taṣawwuf* of Kalābādhī. I made a copy of this manuscript, and during a winter in Egypt I was able to collate this copy with two other much older manuscripts of the work which are preserved in the Royal Library at Cairo. Later my attention was drawn to a fourth copy, contained in the library of the late Timur Pasha, which had then just been made available to the public. These four manuscripts[1] were the basis of an edition of the text which, through the generous enterprise of the well-known Cairo publisher, Khangi, was produced in the summer of 1934.

This edition, based as it is largely on manuscripts not generally available to European scholars, was not intended as a final text of the work, but rather as a basis for a future completely critical edition: for I am aware —through the kindly advice of Dr Ritter[2]—that there are in Turkey manuscripts of the work which antedate considerably those used in my edition;[3] moreover, this edition overlooks the European manuscripts,[4] which are however of little importance compared with those

[1] Sigla: M = Cairo *Taṣawwuf* 66 M, dated 779/1377.
N = Nicholson Collection, incomplete and undated.
Q = Cairo *Taṣawwuf* 170 M, dated 787/1385.
T = Timur Pasha *Taṣawwuf* 266, undated.

[2] *Vid. Orientalia* I (Istanbuler Mitteilungen 1), pp. 78–82.

[3] Carullah 955, dated 623/1226; Carullah 1028 (with anonymous commentary), dated 756/1355; Çelebi Abdullah 176 (with commentary of Qōnawī), dated 822/1419.

[4] Berlin 3027 = B; Vienna 1888 = V; Bodleian II 253; India Office (Delhi Arabic) 1847; I.O. (Delhi Persian) 999; Paris Persian 80; Berlin Persian 246.

in Turkey. If the occasion ever arises, and a text with full *apparatus criticus* is planned, it is hoped that the Cairo edition will serve as a useful point of departure.

In making this translation of the text, I have derived considerable help from the commentary of Qōnawī, which the Director of the Nationalbibliothek of Vienna kindly lent for my use in the India Office; with this I compared the Berlin abstract of Manūfī, generously put at my disposal by the Director of the Preussische Staatsbibliothek. My version is, however, by strict principle independent of inspired comment, and seeks to provide as literal a rendering of the original as English prose-style will permit. It will be observed that the poetical citations, which are numerous, have been translated into English verse: it would surely be an offence against taste, in a version of a work of considerable literary merits which aims at appealing to a public largely unfamiliar with the Arabic language, to furnish a pedantic prose dissection of these mystical poems, some of which are of striking beauty. The scholar will, I believe, find these versions so literal that he will be satisfied that they are an accurate reflection of their originals: the general reader will, I hope, be able to catch through them some glimpse, however faint, of the spirit breathed into them by their composers.

Little is known concerning the author of this treatise, Abū Bakr ibn Abī Isḥāq Muḥammad ibn Ibrāhīm ibn Ya'qūb al-Bukhārī al-Kalābādhī.[1] His

[1] Various forms are given for his patronymics: (i) Muḥammad b. Isḥāq ('Abd al-Ḥayy, *al-Fawā'id al-bahīyah* (Lucknow, 1293/1876), p. 65); (ii) Muḥammad b. Isḥāq b. Ibrāhīm (Ahlwardt, *Verzeichniss*, III, p. 93; Brockelmann, *Geschichte*, I, p. 200; I.O. (Delhi Persian) MS. 999, fol. 2*b*); (iii) Muḥammad b. Ibrāhīm (Ḥājjī Khalīfah, II, pp. 20, 316); (iv) Muḥammad b. Ibrāhīm b. Ya'qūb (Ethé, *Catalogue of Persian Manuscripts in the India Office*, I, p. 302; Flügel, *Die arabischen...Handschriften*, III, p. 315; I.O. (Delhi Arabic) MS. 1847, fol. 1*a*). The last form would appear to be correct.

nisbah refers to Kalābā<u>dh</u>, a quarter of Bu<u>kh</u>ārā,[1] and it is to be presumed that Bu<u>kh</u>ārā was his native city; and in fact it was in Bu<u>kh</u>ārā that he was buried.[2] It is stated by ʿAbd al-Ḥayy al-La<u>kh</u>nawī, who includes him in his list of famous Ḥanafī lawyers, that he studied *fiqh* under one Muḥammad ibn Faḍl.[3] Concerning the date of his death some confusion exists among the authorities. Ḥājjī <u>Kh</u>alīfah in two places[4] gives the year 380/990, and this is the date generally accepted.[5] Dārā <u>Sh</u>ikūh[6] states that he died on Friday the 19th of Jumādā I, 380, adding however that "some say 384, some 385". A note in the India Office (Delhi Arabic) MS. 1847 reads, "he died in 380, or it is said 384 or 385".[7] If reliance may be placed on Dārā <u>Sh</u>ikūh's authority, then it must be concluded that the correct date for the death of Kalābā<u>dh</u>ī is 385/995, for this is the only year in that decade in which 19 Jumādā I fell on a Friday.[8]

One other work of Kalābā<u>dh</u>ī, apart from the *Taʿarruf*, has been preserved, namely, *Baḥr al-fawāʾid fī maʿānī al-a<u>kh</u>bār*.[9] This is, however, a work of an entirely different character, for it is a commentary on 222 selected Traditions.[10]

1 Cf. Veth, *Lexicon geographicum*, II, p. 506; Yāqūt, *Muʿjam al-buldān* (Cairo, 1324/1906), VII, p. 269.

2 Dārā <u>Sh</u>ikūh, *Safīnat al-awliyā* (I.O. MS. 660), fol. 101*a*.

3 *Loc. cit.*

4 II, pp. 20, 316.

5 Brockelmann states 380/990 or 390, Nicholson (*Literary History of the Arabs*, p. 338) gives *circa* 1000 A.D.

6 *Loc. cit.* This date is also given in a note on fol. 2*b* of I.O. (Delhi Persian) MS. 999.

7 Fol. 1*a*; a similar statement appears to be made in Brussa MS. Eşrefzade 161.

8 In 377 also, but this would be too early.

9 Ḥ. <u>Kh</u>. II, 1671. MSS. at London (School of Oriental Studies 200), Paris (5855) and Istanbul (Yeni Cami 247, Fatih 697, etc.).

10 Kalābā<u>dh</u>ī should not therefore be confused with his namesake, the well-known traditionist Abū Naṣr Aḥmad b. Muḥammad al-Kalābā<u>dh</u>ī, author of a biographical dictionary of the authorities quoted in the *Ṣaḥīḥ* of Bu<u>kh</u>ārī: see Yāqūt, *loc. cit.*; Ibn al-ʿImād, *<u>Sh</u>ad<u>h</u>arāt al-<u>dh</u>ahab* (Cairo, 1350/1931), III, p. 151.

It is upon the *Ta'arruf* that Kalābā<u>dh</u>ī's fame rests. This treatise was soon accepted as an authoritative text-book on Ṣūfī doctrine, and commentaries were written upon it by a number of eminent writers. The esteem in which it was held by so illustrious an author as Suhrawardī Maqtūl (d. 587/1191) is indicated by his much-quoted saying, "But for the *Ta'arruf* we should not have known of Ṣūfism".[1] Ḥājjī <u>Kh</u>alīfah, in his account of the book,[2] enumerates the following four commentaries: (1) by Kalābā<u>dh</u>ī himself, entitled *Ḥusn al-taṣarruf*; (2) by 'Abdullāh ibn Muḥammad al-Anṣārī al-Harawī (d. 481/1088); (3) by 'Alā al-Dīn 'Alī ibn Ismā'īl al-Qōnawī (d. 729/1329); (4) by Ismā'īl ibn Muḥammad ibn 'Abdillāh al-Mustamlī. It is quite evident that Ḥājjī <u>Kh</u>alīfah errs in ascribing the *Ḥusn al-taṣarruf* to Kalābā<u>dh</u>ī: for this is the title of Qōnawī's commentary, as Ḥājjī K<u>h</u>alīfah recognises in another place.[3] Possibly the error arose from the fact that Kalābā<u>dh</u>ī does in fact provide a commentary in some passages on difficult sayings or verses which he quotes.[4] The commentary of Anṣārī appears to have been lost, unless indeed it is to be identified with the "anonymous commentary".[5] Of Qōnawī's commentary several manuscripts have survived, notably that at Vienna, a late but accurate copy; and from this extracts were made by 'Alī ibn Aḥmad al-Manūfī (*c.* 880/1475), the only copy of which is preserved at Berlin.[6] The commentary of

[1] This saying is quoted in the preface of the anonymous commentary (Bodleian II 253), and is there attributed to Suhrawardī, thus giving rise to the misconception that that commentary is the work of Suhrawardī himself: so Massignon (*Bibliographie hallagienne*, no. 143) writes of a "1re récension de Sohrawardî Maqtoûl". See Ritter, *loc. cit.* Ḥ. <u>Kh</u>. (II, p. 316) quotes this saying in an anonymous form.

[2] II, 3083.

[3] II, 3033, cf. III, 4496.

[4] Cf. pp. 61, 75, 76, etc. (Arabic text). Flügel is puzzled by this slip of Ḥ. <u>Kh</u>., and supposes (*op. cit.* III, p. 316, n. 1) that the Vienna manuscript contains the commentary of Kalābā<u>dh</u>ī himself, with additions (Zusätze) by Qōnawī.

[5] See Ritter, *loc. cit.*

[6] Ahlwardt 3027.

Mustamlī, which must have been written before the year 710/1310,[1] likewise survives:[2] it is written in Persian, with the original text of Kalābādhī followed by a Persian translation. Of this commentary also an abstract was made, by an anonymous writer: this abstract survives,[3] and contains the Persian translation and a shortened commentary only, except that in the verse passages the Arabic text is also given.

A lengthy quotation from the *Ta'arruf* occurs in the *Mashra' al-khuṣūṣ*, a commentary on the *Nuṣūṣ* of Qōnawī, by 'Alī ibn Aḥmad al-Mahā'imī (d. 835/1431);[4] while copious extracts are incorporated by Suyūṭī (d. 911/1505) in his *Ta'yīd al-ḥaqīqat al-'alīyah*.[5] Selections from the *Ta'arruf*, illustrating the doctrines of Ḥallāj, were published by Massignon in his *Textes Hallajiens*, pp. 10–22.[6]

It may be said that, after the *Risālah* of Qushayrī and the *Qūt al-qulūb* of Makkī, Kalābādhī's *Ta'arruf* was esteemed by the Arabs, especially the Ṣūfīs themselves, as the most valuable compendium of Ṣūfism written. It is not necessary to look far to discover the reason for this. In the first place, it is a short work, compared even with the *Risālah* and the *Qūt al-qulūb*, and the Arab ever asserts his love of brevity, though he may on occasions be excessively prolix. Secondly—and this is a major consideration—the author's chief purpose in writing the book is to demonstrate the essential ortho-

[1] For this is the date of composition of the abstract: cf. I.O. (Delhi Persian) MS. 999, fol. 6 *b*; Pertsch, *Pers. Handschriften... Berlin*, p. 246.

[2] Carullah 1027, Şehit Ali 1231, Riza Paşa 875, Paris (Blochet) 80 (incomplete).

[3] Berlin Persian 246, I.O. (Delhi Persian) 999.

[4] I.O. (Delhi Arabic) 1811, fol. 10 *a*.

[5] Cairo edition of 1352/1934, pp. 10, 28, 51, etc. The commentary of Qōnawī is also quoted, pp. 86, 91. Suyūṭī does not refer to Kalābādhī by name, but styles him simply *Ṣāḥib al-ta'arruf*.

[6] Appendix to *Essai sur les origines du lexique technique* (Paris, 1922).

doxy of the Ṣūfī position. It is not for nothing that he sets, in the very forefront of his work, a lengthy and perhaps tedious enumeration of the central doctrines of Islam. To appreciate the significance of this portion of the book, it is only necessary to compare it closely with the *Fiqh Akbar*, II, which Wensinck[1] has shown to be the work of a Ḥanbalī theologian of not later than the tenth century A.D. Not only does Kalābā<u>dh</u>ī follow closely the order of the articles contained in that "creed", but so striking are the verbal correspondences[2] between the two that it is impossible to doubt that our author is quoting directly from that document. Ṣūfism was passing through a grave crisis, and was in danger of being outlawed, especially since the execution of Ḥallāj in 922, an event which may well have taken place in Kalābā<u>dh</u>ī's childhood:[3] our author musters all his

[1] *The Muslim Creed* (Cambridge 1932), p. 246.

[2] Compare for example the following passages: "Allah the exalted is one.... He has been from eternity and will be to eternity with His names and qualities.... Those which belong to His essence are: life, power, knowledge, speech, hearing, sight and will. Those which belong to His action are: creating, sustaining, producing, renewing, making, and so on" (*Fiqh Akbar*, II, art. 2, p. 188). "The Ṣūfīs are agreed that God is One, Alone, Single, Eternal, Everlasting, Knowing, Powerful, Living, Hearing, Seeing, Strong, Majestic.... Desirous, Speaking, Creating, Sustaining...that since eternity He has not ceased to continue with His names and attributes.... They are agreed that God has real qualities, and that He is qualified by them, these being: knowledge, strength, power, might, mercy, wisdom, majesty, omnipotence, eternity, life, desire, will and speech" (*Ta'arruf*, trans. pp. 14, 16). Compare again: "The Kuran is the speech of Allah, written in the copies, preserved in the memories, recited by the tongues" (*Fiqh Akbar*, II, art. 3, p. 189). "They are agreed that the Qur'ān is the real word of God...that it is recited by our tongues, written in our books, and preserved in our breasts" (*Ta'arruf*, p. 21). These correspondences might be many times multiplied. The whole of this section of the *Ta'arruf* reads like an amplification of the *Fiqh Akbar*, interspersed with quotations from Ṣūfī authorities to prove their adherence to each point.

[3] It is striking to note that Kalābā<u>dh</u>ī, as Massignon has pointed out (*Bibliographie hallagienne*, no. 143), never refers to Ḥallāj by name. He always refers to him as "one of the great

forces to prove that the true doctrine of the Ṣūfīs, so far from being heretical, is actually conformable with the strictest standards of orthodoxy. It is this conscious motive on his part that gives the work a value greater even than that of the other famous Ṣūfī *compendia*, of Qushayrī, Makkī, Sarrāj and Hujwīrī: while these four great books may be richer mines of information for the historian of Ṣūfism, they could hardly, with perhaps the exception of the *Qūt al-qulūb*, have had so determining an influence as the *Ta'arruf* in winning for Ṣūfism official recognition by orthodox Islam. In this sense Kalābādhī blazes a path which was subsequently to be followed by the Ṣūfī who was the greatest theologian of all, Ghazālī (d. 505/1111), whose *Iḥyā* finally reconciled scholastic and mystic.

The "Doctrine of the Ṣūfīs"[1] falls naturally into five parts.

(I) Prooemium, chapters 1–4. In these opening chapters the author provides a general introduction to the subject, discusses the meaning and proposed derivations of the term Ṣūfī, and enumerates the names of the great Ṣūfīs: in this list many distinguished persons appear, beginning with 'Alī and his sons, and including Ḥasan al-Baṣrī, Mālik ibn Dīnār, Fuḍayl ibn 'Iyād, and Sufyān al-Thawrī, men whose orthodoxy and authority had never been impugned. The prooemium itself is a classical piece, meditating on a theme much

Ṣūfīs" (see this translation, p. 15, n. 2), except that twice, towards the end (pp. 150, 152), he calls him Abu 'l-Mughīth. It is not without significance that Kalābādhī, in his supremely important chapter on Divine Unity, illustrates his discourse with but one quotation, and that a lengthy passage taken from Ḥallāj (pp. 15–16). As Massignon has observed (*Passion*, p. 338, quoting Jāmī, *Nafaḥāt al-uns*, p. 173), Kalābādhī was a disciple of Fāris—from whom he quotes as a first-hand authority (cf. pp. 81, 88, 91)—and Fāris was a vigorous defender of Ḥallāj. Ṣūfīs would recognise these quotations as coming from Ḥallāj: meanwhile Kalābādhī is doing missionary propaganda on his behalf.

[1] The full title may be translated, "An Enquiry into the true nature of Ṣūfī doctrine".

used by the Ṣūfīs—the former glory of Islam, and the decay into which it has fallen in the writer's day. The first to use this theme among the Ṣūfīs, so far as I am aware, was Muḥāsibī, in the introduction to his *Naṣā'iḥ*.[1]

(II) Chapters 5–30. This section is a statement of the tenets of Islam, as accepted by the Ṣūfīs: the purpose of this section, as I have pointed out, is to prove that Ṣūfism as a system lies within and not without the bounds of orthodoxy. Kalābādhī's words in this connection are significant: "These are the true doctrines of the Ṣūfīs...let any man study and examine their discourse and books, and he will know that what we have related is true. Indeed, but for our being loath to make a long discussion, we would have quoted chapter and verse from their books for every point we have mentioned, for all this is not set down sufficiently clearly in the books".[2] It should be noted that chapters 21 and 22 (Of Gnosis, Of the Nature of Gnosis) appear to be misplaced in this section, and more properly belong to the third part.

[1] MS. Brit. Mus. Or. 7900, foll. 1–2: "It hath come to pass in our days, that this community is divided into more than seventy sects: of these, one only is in the way of salvation, and for the rest, God knows best concerning them. Now I have not ceased, not so much as one moment of my life, to consider well the differences into which the community has fallen, and to search after the clear way and the true path; and thereunto I have sought of both theory and practice, and looked for guidance to the road of the world to come in the directing of the theologians. Moreover, I have studied much of the doctrine of God Most High, with the interpretation of the lawyers, and reflected upon the various conditions of the community, and considered its divers doctrines and sayings. Of all this I understood as much as was appointed for me to understand: and I saw that their divergence was as it were a deep sea, wherein many had been drowned, and but a small band therefrom escaped; and I saw every party of them asserting that salvation was to be found in following them, and that he would perish who opposed them." This passage, as Massignon has pointed out (*Essai*, p. 216), is strongly reminiscent of the *Munqidh* of Ghazālī.

[2] Pp. 73–4 (translation).

(III) Chapters 31–51. This is a discussion of the various stations of the Ṣūfīs, such as fear, hope, love, etc. The author illustrates his remarks with copious quotations, both prose and verse.

(IV) Chapters 52–63. This section, which is perhaps the most important of the book, discusses the "technical terms" of the Ṣūfīs, that is, the expressions used by them to designate the true mystical experience, Union with God. Kalābā<u>dh</u>ī warns his readers[1] that this discussion only touches on the actual meanings of the terms employed, for the experiences themselves cannot possibly be described in words. He hazards the important conjecture that all these terms—union, separation, passing-away, abiding—really describe one and the same experience.[2]

(V) Chapters 64–75. The book concludes with descriptions of the various phenomena of Ṣūfism, and of the miraculous dispensations accorded to the Ṣūfīs by God. Kalābā<u>dh</u>ī thus produces his material evidence to supplement the purely theoretical discussion which has gone before, and hopes thereby to prove his assertion that the Ṣūfīs are truly men of God.

The value of the *Taʿarruf*, as a primary source, is most fairly assessed by analysing the sayings and anecdotes of Ṣūfīs preserved in it, and estimating what proportion of them are found in the other *compendia*, and for what proportion Kalābā<u>dh</u>ī is, or appears to be, a unique authority. I have taken for this purpose the famous Ṣūfī <u>Kh</u>arrāz as a typical example. Kalābā<u>dh</u>ī mentions his name ten times: in three passages[3] he makes general statements about him; in five[4] he quotes sayings; in two[5] he relates anecdotes. The general statements may be regarded as inadmissible as evidence: one of them at least occurs in a later work.[6] All five

[1] P. 104. [2] P. 125. [3] Pp. 11, 22, 96 (Arabic text).
[4] Pp. 40, 71, 72, 90, 94 (text). [5] Pp. 115, 116 (text).
[6] P. 11: "<u>Kh</u>arrāz is called the Tongue of Ṣūfism". This statement is reproduced by ʿAṭṭār, *Ta<u>dh</u>kirat al-awliyā*, II, p. 40.

sayings appear to be original to Kalābādhī. Of the two anecdotes one is recounted by other authorities.[1] If this example may be accepted as representative, it is clear that the *Ta'arruf* must be assigned very high value as an authority: it is not too much to say, as Nicholson has said,[2] that it is one of eight books whose study is the foundation for a history of Ṣūfism, when that history comes to be written.

I cannot end these remarks without expressing my sincere thanks to Professor Nicholson, who read this translation in manuscript and has made valuable suggestions; to Dr Ritter, who provided me with precise information concerning the Istanbul manuscripts; and to the Syndics of the Cambridge University Press, who have generously undertaken the risks which unfortunately are inseparable from the publishing of works of this kind.

A. J. A.

WALLINGTON,
June 1935.

[1] P. 116. This story is also told by Ibn 'Asākir (*al-Ta'rīkh al-kabīr*, I, p. 431) and 'Aṭṭār (*op. cit.* II, p. 42).

[2] Introduction, p. ii, to his edition of the *Kitāb al-Luma'* of Sarrāj.

PROOEMIUM

In the Name of God, the Merciful, the Compassionate!

Praise belongs to God, Who by His magnificence is veiled from the perception of the eyes, and by His glory and might is exalted above the attainment of the thoughts; Whose essence, being unique, does not resemble the essences of created beings, and Whose qualities are far removed from the qualities of creatures born in time. He is the Ancient Who has never ceased, the Abiding Who will never pass away: high set is He beyond all likenesses, opposites, and forms. By His marks and signs He guides His creation to (a knowledge of) His unity, and He makes Himself known to His saints through His names, attributes and qualities: for He brings near to Him their secret parts, and inclines their hearts towards Him; with His kindliness He advances upon them, and in His lovingkindness He draws them unto Him, having cleansed their inward parts from the impurities of the flesh,[1] and exalted their faculties above associating with the things that perish. He has chosen from among them those whom He wished to be His apostles, and elected those whom He desired to be His ambassadors and the recipients of His revelation: He has sent down upon them books containing His command and prohibition, giving promises to those who obeyed, and threats to such as disobeyed. He has made clear their superiority over all mankind, and raised up their ranks beyond the reach of every person of whatever consequence.

With Muḥammad (upon whom be blessing and peace!) God has sealed them, ordaining faith in him, and resignation: for his religion is the best of religions, and his community the best of communities; his law

[1] Lit. "souls".

can never be abrogated, and there is no community after his community.

Among them God has placed men chosen and elect, excellent and pious: God's better portion came to them betimes. For God bound them with the word of fear, and turned their souls away from this world. They were true in their endeavours, and they attained the sciences of study;[1] their dealings therein were sincere, and they were granted the sciences of inheritance;[2] their secret hearts were pure, and they were ennobled with true intuition.[3] Their feet were firm, their understandings were clean, their beacons were bright: they had understanding of God, and journeyed unto God, and turned away from what is other than God. Their lights pierced the veils, their secret parts moved round the Throne of God: very highly were they esteemed by Him Who sits upon the Throne, and their eyes were blind to all beneath the Throne. They were spiritual bodies, being upon earth celestial, and with creation divines: silent and meditative, absent (from men) but present (with God), kings in rags,[4] outcasts from every tribe, possessors of all virtues and lights of all guidance; their ears attentive, their hearts pure, their qualities concealed;[5] chosen, Ṣūfīs, illuminated, pure. These were deposited by God among His creation, and chosen out of those whom God made: they were His testaments to His Prophet, and His secrets entrusted to His Chosen One. During his lifetime they were the people of his bench,[6] and after his death they were the best of his community. Thereafter the first did not fail to call the second, and the predecessor the successor, with the

[1] Sc. of the Qur'ān.

[2] I.e. the Traditions (*ḥadīth*) and stories of the saints (*akhbār*).

[3] Sc. the mystical knowledge born of personal experience.

[4] The "Buddha" tradition in Ṣūfism, as with Ibrāhīm ibn Adham.

[5] As with the Malāmatīs, in order to incur the contempt of men.

[6] *Ṣuffah*, cited by some native authorities as the derivation of the name *ṣūfī* (cf. *infra*, p. 9).

tongue of his work,[1] which freed him of the necessity of speech. But then desire diminished and purpose flagged: and with this came the spate of questions and answers, books and treatises; the inner meanings were known to those who wrote, and the breasts (of those who read) were receptive to understand them.[2] Finally, the meaning departed, and the name remained, the substance vanished and the shadow took its place: realisation became an ornament, and verification a decoration. He who knew not (the truth) pretended to possess it, he who had never so much as described it adorned himself with it: he who had it much upon his tongue denied it with his acts, and he who displayed it in his exposition concealed it by his true conduct. That which was not of it was introduced into it, that which was not in it was ascribed to it: its truth was made false, and he who knew it was called ignorant. But he who had experienced (the truth) drew apart, being jealous for it: he who had described it was silent, being envious for it. So the hearts (of men) fled from it, and the souls departed; science and its people, exposition and its practice, vanished; the ignorant became the scientists, and the scientists became the guides.

It was this that provoked me to sketch in my present book a description of their way, an exposition of their manner and character. Herein I have discoursed upon their doctrines concerning the Unity and Qualities of God, and all other matters therewith connected, as to which any doubt has arisen among those who did not know their dogmas and did not study under their Shaykhs. I have revealed in the language of science all that can be revealed, and described with outward exposition[3] all that is meet to be described, so that it may be understood by those who have not understood their allusions, and comprehended by those who have

[1] Sc. the example of his life.
[2] This refers to the period of Muḥāsibī, Junayd, etc.
[3] As opposed to the inner reality, which is far higher.

not comprehended their expressions. By this I have endeavoured to defend them against the envy of the envious, and the evil interpretation of the ignorant: while at the same time this book will serve as a guide to those who desire to tread God's path, and have need of God for the attainment of the realisation of this. This I have done, having first thoroughly studied the writings of those who are versed in this matter, and sifted the stories of those who have attained a true realisation of it: moreover I have associated with such men, and questioned them. And I have called this book the "Book of Knowledge of the Doctrine of the Ṣūfīs", to indicate the purport of its contents. Of God I seek help, and in Him is my trust: His Prophet I bless, making him my mediator. No power or help is there, save with God!

Chapter I

HOW THE ṢŪFĪS ACCOUNT FOR THEIR BEING CALLED ṢŪFĪS

Some say: "The Ṣūfīs were only named Ṣūfīs because of the purity (*ṣafā*) of their hearts and the cleanliness of their acts (*āthār*)." Bishr ibn al-Ḥārith said: "The Ṣūfī is he whose heart is sincere (*ṣafā*) towards God." Another said: "The Ṣūfī is he whose conduct towards God is sincere, and towards whom God's blessing is sincere." Certain of them have said: "They were only called Ṣūfīs because they are in the first rank (*ṣaff*) before God, through the elevation of their desires towards Him, the turning of their hearts unto Him, and the staying of their secret parts before Him." Others have said: "They were only called Ṣūfīs because their qualities resembled those of the people of the Bench (*ṣuffah*), who lived in the time of God's Prophet (God's blessing and peace be upon him!)." Others have said: "They were only named Ṣūfīs because of their habit of wearing wool (*ṣūf*)."

Those who relate them to the Bench and to wool express the outward aspect of their conditions: for they were people who had left this world, departed from their homes, fled from their companions. They wandered about the land, mortifying the carnal desires, and making naked the body: they took of this world's goods only so much as is indispensable for covering the nakedness and allaying hunger. For departing from their homes they were called "strangers"; for their many journeyings they were called "travellers"; for their travelling in deserts, and taking refuge in caves at times of necessity, certain people of the country (*diyār*) called them "*shikaftīs*", for the word "*shikaft*" in their language means "cavern" or "cave".[1] The Syrians called them "starvers", because they only took as much food as would keep up their strength in time of necessity. So the Prophet (God's blessing and peace be upon him!) said: "Sufficient for the son of Adam are such morsels as will keep up his strength." Sarī al-Saqaṭī described them thus: "Their food is the food of the sick, their sleep is the sleep of the drowned, their speech is the speech of fools." Because they were devoid of possessions they were called "paupers". One of them was asked: "Who is a Ṣūfī?" He replied: "He who neither possesses nor is possessed." By this he meant that he is not the slave of desire. Another said: "(The Ṣūfī is) he who possesses nothing, or, if he possesses anything, spends it." Because of their clothes and manner of dressing they were called Ṣūfīs: for they did not put on raiment soft to touch or beautiful to behold, to give delight to the soul; they only clothed themselves in order to hide their nakedness, contenting themselves with rough haircloth and coarse wool.

Now these were in fact the conditions under which the people of the Bench lived, in the time of the Prophet (God's blessing and peace be upon him!): for they were strangers, poor, exiles, having been driven out of their abodes and possessions. Abū Hurayrah and Fuḍālah ibn 'Ubayd described them as follows: "They faint of hunger, so that the Bedouins suppose them to be mad." Their clothing was of wool, so that when any of them sweated, they gave off an odour like that of a sheep caught in the rain. This, indeed, is how they are described by some. 'Uyaynah ibn Ḥiṣn said to the Prophet (God's blessing and peace be upon him!): "The smell of these men distresses me. Does it not distress thee?" Wool is also the dress of the Prophets and the garb of the Saints. Abū Mūsā al-Ash'arī relates the following of the Prophet (God's blessing and peace be upon him!): "There passed by the rock at Rawḥā

[1] So in Persian.

seventy prophets bare of foot, clad in the '*abā*,[1] repairing to the Ancient House."[2] Al-Ḥasan al-Baṣrī said: "Jesus (peace be upon him!) used to wear haircloth, eat the fruit of the trees, and spend the night wherever he happened to find himself." Abū Mūsā al-Ash'arī said: "The Prophet (God's blessing and peace be upon him!) used to wear wool, ride asses, and accept the invitation of the insignificant (to eat with them)." Al-Ḥasan al-Baṣrī said: "I have known of seventy of those who fought at Badr, whose clothes were only of wool."

Now as this sect had the same qualities as the people of the Bench, as we have described, being clothed and apparelled like them, they were called "*ṣuffīyah ṣūfīyah*". Those who relate them to the Bench and the First Rank indicate their secret hearts and inward parts: for when a man abandons this world, and is abstemious therein, and turns aside therefrom, God purifies (*ṣaffā*) his conscience (*sirr*) and illuminates his heart. The Prophet (God's blessing and peace be upon him!) has said: "When light enters into the heart, it is expanded and dilated." They said: "And what is the sign of that, O Messenger of God?" He replied: "Shunning the abode of deceit, turning to the abode of eternity, and making ready for death before death descends." So the Prophet (God's blessing, etc.) stated that, if a man shuns this world, God will illuminate his heart. The Prophet (God's blessing, etc.) asked Ḥārithah: "What is the reality of thy faith?" He answered: "I have inclined my soul away from this world, I have fasted by day, and kept vigil at night: and it is as though I behold the Throne of my Lord coming forth, and as if I behold the people of Paradise visiting one another, and the people of Hell at enmity with one another."[3] Thus he informs us that, when he inclined away from this world, God illuminated his heart, so that what was (normally)

[1] A woollen garment. [2] Sc. the Ka'bah.

[3] This version exhibits some variants from the usual form: *vid. infr.*

unseen to him assumed a place in his vision. The Prophet also said: "If any man wishes to behold a servant whose heart God has illuminated, let him look upon Ḥārithah." Because of these qualities, this sect has also been called "illuminated" (*nūrīyah*). This description also befits the people of the Bench; God Most High says: "Therein are men who love to be clean."[1] (This means), the outward parts are clean of defilements, and the inward parts of wicked thoughts. God Most High also says: "Men whom neither merchandise nor selling divert from the remembrance of God."[2] Moreover, because of the purity of their consciences, their intuition (*firāsah*) is true. Abū Umāmah relates that the Prophet said: "Fear the intuition of the believer, for he beholds with the light of God." Abū Bakr al-Ṣiddīq said: "It was put into my heart that he was the offspring of Khārijah's daughter"; and it was so.[3] The Prophet said: "Truth speaks on the tongue of 'Umar." Uways al-Qaranī said to Harim ibn Ḥaiyān, when the latter greeted him, "And on thee be peace, O Harim son of Ḥaiyān!"—and yet he had never seen him before that moment. Then he added: "My spirit recognised thy spirit." Abū 'Abdillāh al-Anṭākī said: "When ye associate with the people of sincerity, associate with them in sincerity: for they are the spies of the hearts, entering into your consciences, and emerging from your inward desires." Now, if a man is of this description, if his conscience is pure, his heart is clean, his breast illuminated, then certainly he is in the first rank: for these are the qualities of the leaders.[4] The Prophet said: "There will enter Paradise of my community seventy thousand without reckoning." Then he went on, and described them:

[1] S. ix. 109.
[2] S. xxiv. 37.
[3] Abū Bakr married the daughter of Khārijah, with whom he was joined in "brotherhood"; see Muir, *Life of Muḥammad*, 159, n. 2.
[4] *Sābiq*, the term here used, refers to the earliest converts to Islam.

"Men who neither practise magic nor seek to be charmed, who neither brand nor are branded, but put their trust in their Lord."[1] Further, because of the purity of their consciences, and the dilation of their breasts, and the brightness of their hearts, they had a perfect gnosis of God, and did not have recourse to secondary causes (*asbāb*): they put their faith in God Most High, and trusted Him, being satisfied with His decree. All these qualities, and all the meanings contained in these terms, are united in the names and nicknames given to this people: these expressions are exact, and these derivations come near to the truth. Even though these words vary in outward appearance, yet the meanings behind them are identical. If the term (*ṣūfī*) were derived from *ṣafā* (purity) or *ṣafwah* (choice), the correct form would be *ṣafawīyah*; while if it were referred to *ṣaff* (rank) or *ṣuffah* (bench), it would be *ṣaffīyah* or *ṣuffīyah*. It is, of course, possible (in the former case) that the *waw* has been transferred to come before the *fā*, so giving *ṣūfīyah*; or (if the latter derivation be accepted), that it is simply redundant, being inserted into the word through common practice.[2] If, however, the derivation from *ṣūf* (wool) be accepted, the word is correct and the expression sound from the grammatical point of view, while at the same time it has all the (necessary) meanings, such as withdrawal from the world, inclining the soul away from it, leaving all settled abodes, keeping constantly to travel, denying the carnal soul its pleasures, purifying the conduct, cleansing the conscience, dilation of the breast, and the quality of leadership.[3] Bundār ibn al-Ḥusayn said: "The Ṣūfī is the man whom God has chosen for Himself, rendering him a sincere affection (*ṣāfā*), and setting him free from his carnal soul, and not allowing him

[1] This version exhibits slight variants from the usual form cf. Muslim, *Ṣaḥīḥ* (Cairo 1347), III, p. 90.

[2] Lit. "from being passed from tongue to tongue."

[3] Cf. p. 4, n. 4.

any more to labour to undue fatigue under any pretext.[1] So he is befriended (*ṣūfī*): as parallels one may cite *'ūfī* (he is preserved), that is, God has preserved him and therefore he is preserved; *kūfī* (he is recompensed), that is, God has recompensed him and therefore he is recompensed; and *jūzī* (he is rewarded), that is, God has rewarded him (and therefore he is rewarded).[2] What God has done to him is manifest in his name, although God is entirely independent of him." Abū 'Alī al-Rudhabārī, being asked what a Ṣūfī is, replied: "One who wears wool over (his) purity, gives his lust the taste of tyranny, and, having overthrown the world, journeys in the pathway of the Chosen One."[3] Sahl ibn 'Abdillāh al-Tustarī gave the following answer to the same question: "One who is clean of impurity, and full of meditation; who is cut off from humanity for God's sake, and in whose eyes gold and mud are equal."[4] Abu 'l-Ḥusayn al-Nūrī, being asked what Ṣūfism is, replied: "Abandoning all the portion of the carnal soul." Al-Junayd was asked the same question, and said: "It is the purification of the heart from associating with created beings, separation from natural characteristics, suppression of human qualities, avoiding the temptations of the carnal soul, taking up the qualities of the spirit, attachment to the sciences of reality, using what is more proper to the eternal, counselling all the community, being truly faithful to God, and following the Prophet according to the Law."

Yūsuf ibn al-Ḥusayn said: "There is in every community a chosen band, and they are the agents[5] of God, concealed by Him from His creation: if there be any

[1] Sc. in affairs not concerned with the path to God.

[2] A laboured attempt to construe the term *ṣūfī* as a passive of the verb *ṣāfā*.

[3] Sc. Muḥammad.

[4] For another version of this saying, *vid. infr.*, where it is attributed to Ḥārithah.

[5] Lit. "deposit".

such in this community, they are the Ṣūfīs." A certain man said to Sahl ibn 'Abdillāh al-Tustarī: "With whom shall I associate of the various sects of mankind?" He replied: "Occupy thyself with the Ṣūfīs, for they find nothing objectionable, but provide a spiritual interpretation (*ta'wīl*) for every act, and will make excuses for thee whatever thy state (*ḥāl*) may be."[1] Yūsuf ibn al-Ḥusayn tells us that he asked Dhu 'l-Nūn: "With whom shall I associate?" He answered: "With him who possesses nothing, and does not disapprove of any state thou happenest to be in; who does not change when thou changest, even though that change be great: for the more violently thou changest, the greater is thy need of him."[2] Dhu 'l-Nūn also said: "I saw a woman in one of the coasts of Syria, and said to her, 'Whence comest thou (God have mercy on thee)?' She replied: 'From people whose flanks shrink from beds.' I said: 'And whither intendest thou?' She answered 'Unto men whom neither merchandise nor selling diverts from the remembrance of God.'[3] I said: 'Describe them.' Then she began to recite:

'Their every purpose is with God united,
Their high ambitions mount to Him alone:
Their troth is to the Lord and Master plighted—
O noble quest, for the Eternal One!

They do not quarrel over this world's pleasure—
Honours, and children, rich and costly gowns,
All greed and appetite! They do not treasure
The life of ease and joy that dwells in towns.

Facing the far and faint horizon yonder
They seek the Infinite, with purpose strong:
They ever tread where desert runnels wander,
And high on towering mountain-tops they throng!'"

[1] This borders on the excesses of the extremists, which the enemies of Ṣūfism were not slow to fasten upon.

[2] The neophyte needs the guidance of a spiritual director to help him through the troublesome difficulties of the first part of his journey: having travelled that way himself, he is well aware of the pitfalls and dangers.

[3] S. xxiv. 37.

Chapter II

A LIST OF THE FAMOUS MEN AMONG THE ṢŪFĪS

The following are the names of those who gave utterance to their sciences and expression to their experiences, that published their stations and described their spiritual states, in word and deed—after the Companions (God's pleasure be upon them!): 'Alī ibn al-Ḥusayn Zayn al-'Ābidīn, his son Muḥammad ibn 'Alī al-Bāqir, and his son Ja'far ibn Muḥammad al-Ṣādiq—these come after 'Alī, Al-Ḥasan, and Al-Ḥusayn (God be well pleased with them!). Then Uways al-Qaranī, Al-Ḥasan ibn Abi 'l-Ḥasan al-Baṣrī, Abū Ḥāzim Salamah ibn Dīnār al-Madanī, Mālik ibn Dīnār, 'Abd al-Wāḥid ibn Zayd, 'Utbah al-Ghulām, Ibrāhīm ibn Adham, Al-Fuḍayl ibn 'Iyāḍ, his son 'Alī ibn al-Fuḍayl, Dāwūd al-Ṭā'ī, Sufyān ibn Sa'īd al-Thawrī, Abū Sulaymān al-Dārānī, his son Sulaymān, Aḥmad ibn al-Ḥawārī al-Dimashqī, Abu 'l-Fayḍ Dhu 'l-Nūn al-Miṣrī, his brother Dhu 'l-Kifl, Sarī ibn al-Mughallis al-Saqaṭī, Bishr ibn al-Ḥārith al-Ḥāfī, Ma'rūf al-Karkhī, Abū Hudhayfah al-Mar'ashī, Muḥammad ibn al-Mubārak al-Ṣūrī, Yūsuf ibn Asbāṭ. Of the people of Khurāsān and Al-Jabal are: Abū Yazīd Ṭayfūr ibn 'Isā al-Bisṭāmī, Abū Ḥafṣ al-Ḥaddād, al-Naysābūrī, Aḥmad ibn Khaḍrūyah al-Balkhī, Sahl ibn 'Abdillāh al-Tustarī, Yūsuf ibn al-Ḥusayn al-Rāzī, Abū Bakr ibn Ṭāhir al-Abharī, 'Alī ibn Sahl ibn al-Azhar al-Iṣfahānī, 'Alī ibn Muḥammad al-Bārizī, Abū Bakr al-Kattānī al-Dīnawarī, Abū Muḥammad ibn al-Ḥasan ibn Muḥammad al-Rajjānī,[1] Al-'Abbās ibn al-Faḍl ibn Qutaybah ibn Manṣūr al-Dīnawarī, Kahmas ibn 'Alī al-Ḥamdānī and Al-Ḥasan ibn 'Alī ibn Yazdāniyār.

[1] So v: cf. Sam'ānī, *Kitāb al-ansāb* (ed. Ellis), f. 248 *b*; Dhahabī, *Mushtabih* (ed. de Jong), p. 218.

Chapter III

A LIST OF THE ṢŪFĪS WHO PUBLISHED THE SCIENCES OF ALLUSION IN BOOKS AND TREATISES

Abu 'l-Qāsim al-Junayd ibn Muḥammad al-Baghdādī, Abu 'l-Ḥusayn Aḥmad ibn Muḥammad ibn 'Abdi 'l-Ṣamad al-Nūrī, Abū Sa'īd Aḥmad ibn 'Īsā al-Kharrāz called the Tongue of Ṣūfism, Abū Muḥammad Ruwaym ibn Muḥammad, Abu 'l-'Abbās Aḥmad ibn 'Aṭā, Abū 'Abdillāh 'Amr ibn 'Uthmān al-Makkī, Abū Ya'qūb Yūsuf ibn Ḥamdān al-Sūsī, Abū Ya'qūb Isḥāq ibn Muḥammad ibn Ayyūb al-Nahrajūrī, Abū Muḥammad al-Ḥasan ibn Muḥammad al-Jurayrī, Abū 'Abdillāh Muḥammad ibn 'Alī al-Kattānī, Abū Isḥāq Ibrāhīm ibn Aḥmad al-Khawwāṣ, Abū 'Alī al-Awzā'ī, Abū Bakr Muḥammad ibn Mūsā al-Wāsiṭī, Abū 'Abdillāh al-Hāshimī, Abū 'Abdillāh Haykal al-Qurashī, Abū 'Alī al-Rudhabārī, Abū Bakr al-Qaḥṭabī, Abū Bakr al-Shiblī called Dulaf ibn Jaḥdar.

Chapter IV

A LIST OF THE ṢŪFĪS WHO HAVE WRITTEN ON CONDUCT

Abū Muḥammad 'Abdullāh ibn Muḥammad al-Anṭākī, Abū 'Abdillāh Aḥmad ibn 'Āṣim al-Anṭākī, 'Abdullāh ibn Khubayq al-Anṭākī, al-Ḥārith ibn Asad al-Muḥāsibī, Yaḥyā bin Mu'ādh al-Rāzī, Abū Bakr Muḥammad ibn 'Umar ibn al-Faḍl al-Warrāq al-Tirmidhī, Abū 'Uthmān Sa'īd ibn Ismā'il al-Rāzī, Abū 'Abdillāh Muḥammad ibn al-Faḍl al-Balkhī, Abū 'Alī al-Jūzajānī, Abu 'l-Qāsim ibn Isḥāq ibn Muḥammad al-Ḥakīm al-Samarqandī. These are the leaders (*a'lām*), remembered and renowned, to whose pre-eminence men have been witnesses. They united the sciences of inheritance with the sciences of acquisition:[1] they heard the Traditions, and combined the law, theology (*kalām*), linguistics, and the science of the Qur'ān; and to this their books and compositions bear witness. We have not mentioned the more recent writers, nor our contemporaries, although they in no way fall short of those whose names we have mentioned in respect of knowledge: for their presence among us renders it unnecessary for us to give an account of them.

Chapter V

THEIR DOCTRINE OF UNITY

The Ṣūfīs are agreed that God is One, Alone, Single, Eternal, Everlasting, Knowing, Powerful, Living, Hearing, Seeing, Strong, Mighty, Majestic, Great, Generous, Clement, Proud, Awful, Enduring, First, God, Lord, Ruler, Master, Merciful, Compassionate, Desirous, Speaking, Creating, Sustaining; that He is qualified with all the attributes wherewith He has qualified Himself, and named with all the names whereby He has named Himself; that since eternity He has not ceased to continue with His names and attributes, without resembling creation in any respect; that His Essence does not resemble the essences, nor His Attribute the attributes; that not one of the terms applied to created beings, and indicating their creation in time, has currency over Him; that He has not ceased to be Leader, Foremost before all things born in time, Existent before everything; that there is no Eternal but He, and no God beside Him; that He is neither

[1] *Vid.* 2, n. 2.

body, nor shape, nor form, nor person, nor element, nor accident; that with Him there is neither junction nor separation, neither movement nor rest, neither augmentation nor decrease; that He has neither parts nor particles nor members nor limbs nor aspects nor places; that He is not affected by faults, nor overcome with slumbers, nor alternated[1] by times, nor specified by allusions; that He is not contained by space, nor affected by time; that He cannot be said to be touched, or to be isolated, or to dwell in places; that He is not compassed by thoughts, nor covered by veils, nor attained by eyes.

One of the great Ṣūfīs[2] said in a discourse of his: "'Before' does not outstrip Him, 'after' does not interrupt Him, 'of' does not vie with Him for precedence, 'from' does not accord with Him, 'to' does not join with Him, 'in' does not inhabit Him, 'when' does not stop[3] Him, 'if' does not consult with Him, 'over' does not overshadow Him, 'under' does not support Him, 'opposite' does not face Him, 'with' does not press Him, 'behind' does not take hold of Him, 'before' does not limit Him, 'previous' does not display Him, 'after' does not cause Him to pass away, 'all' does not unite Him, 'is' does not bring Him to being, 'is not' does not deprive Him of being. Concealment does not veil Him. His pre-existence preceded time, His being preceded not-being, His eternity preceded limit. If thou sayest 'when', His existing has outstripped time; if thou sayest 'before', before is after Him; if thou sayest 'he', 'h' and 'e'[4] are His creation; if thou sayest 'how', His essence is veiled from description; if thou sayest 'where', His being preceded space; if thou sayest 'ipseity' (*mā huwa*), His ipseity

[1] I.e. now active, now inactive.

[2] Sc. Ḥallāj, often so designated in this book. *Vid.* Massignon, *Essai sur les Origines* (Textes Hallajiens), p. 11 (7).

[3] Other MSS. (and Massignon, *loc. cit.*) read "time".

[4] In the original, "h" and "w", sc. *huwa*.

(*huwīyah*) is apart from things. Other than He cannot be qualified by two (opposite) qualities at one time; and yet with Him they do not create opposition. He is hidden in His manifestation, manifest in His concealing. He is outward and inward, near and far; and in this respect He is removed beyond the resemblance of creation. He acts without contact, instructs without meeting, guides without pointing. Desires do not conflict with Him, thoughts do not mingle with Him: His essence is without qualification (*takyīf*), His action without effort (*taklīf*)."

They are agreed that He is neither perceived by the eyes, nor assailed by the thoughts; that His attributes do not change, and that His names do not alter; that He has never ceased thus, and will never cease thus; that He is the First and the Last, the Outward and the Inward; that He is acquainted with everything, that there is nothing like Him, and that He sees and hears.[1]

Chapter VI

THEIR DOCTRINE OF THE ATTRIBUTES

They are agreed that God has real qualities, and that He is qualified by them, these being: knowledge, strength, power, might, mercy, wisdom, majesty, omnipotence, eternity, life, desire, will, and speech. These are neither bodies nor accidents nor elements, even as His essence is neither body nor accident nor element. They also agree that He has hearing, sight, face, and hand, in reality, unlike (ordinary) hearing, sight, hands, and faces. They agree that these are attributes of God, not members or limbs or parts; that they are neither He nor other than He; and that the assertion of their

[1] All these statements have their Qur'ānic sanctions, too numerous to quote here.

being does not imply that He is in need of them, or that He does things with them. Their meaning is the denial of their opposites, the assertion that they both exist in themselves, and subsist through Him. For knowledge does not imply merely the denial of ignorance, nor does power simply connote the denial of weakness: in the one case it is also an assertion of knowledge, in the other an assertion of power.[1] If a man possessed knowledge because he did not possess ignorance, or if he was powerful merely because he lacked weakness, then the very denial of ignorance and weakness would mean that a man has knowledge and power: and so with all the other attributes. The fact that we describe God as having all these attributes in no way bestows any attribute on Him: our description is merely our own attribution, an account we give of an attribute which exists through Him. If any man makes out that his description of God is an attribute of God, without at the same time asserting that God possesses a real attribute, he is a real liar against God, for he makes mention of God with an untrue qualification. This question is not like the question of mentioning: for a person may be "mentioned" through "mention" taking place in someone else, because "mention" is an attribute of the mentioner, not of the person mentioned. The person mentioned is mentioned through the mention of the mentioner: but a person qualified is not qualified by the description of one who describes. Indeed, if the attribution of the describer were an attribute of God, then the attributions of the polytheists and infidels would be His attributes, such as the ascription to Him of a wife, a son, and rivals.[2] But God has cleared Himself of their attribution, when He says: "Celebrated be His praise and exalted be

[1] Sc. it is a positive, not merely a negative, statement.

[2] This laboured passage attempts to make the point that, in the end, God is only truly described by Himself, and that all human attempts to describe Him are necessarily inadequate.

He above what they attribute to Him!"[1] God Most High is qualified through an attribute which subsists through Him, and is not separate from Him. So He says: "And they comprehend not aught of His knowledge."[2] He also says: "He revealed it in His knowledge";[3] and again, "And no female bears or is delivered, except by His knowledge";[4] and again, "Endowed with steady might,[5] Lord of mighty grace;[6] honour belongs wholly to God,[7] possessed of majesty and honour."[8]

They also agree that His attributes are neither diverse nor similar: that His knowledge is not the same as His strength, nor other than His strength; and so with all His attributes, such as hearing, sight, face and hand—His hearing is neither the same as His sight, nor other than His sight, in the same way as His attributes are not He, nor other than He.

They are at variance as to His intervening, coming and descending. The greater part of them hold that these are attributes of His, in so far as they are proper to Him, but that they are not expressed by the greater part of the recitation and relation:[9] nevertheless, one must believe in them unquestioningly. Muḥammad ibn Mūsā al-Wāsiṭī said: "As His essence is not caused, so His attributes are not caused: to attempt to display the eternal is to despair of understanding anything of the realities of the attributes or the subtleties of the essence (of God)." One of the Ṣūfīs gave these attributes an esoteric interpretation, saying: "The meaning of His 'intervening' is, that He brings to Himself whatever He desires; of His 'descending' to a thing, that He advances it towards Him. His 'nearness' means His favour, and His farness means His disdain; and so with all these ambiguous attributes."[10]

[1] S. vi. 100. [2] S. ii. 256. [3] S. iv. 164.
[4] S. xxxv. 12. [5] S. li. 58. [6] S. lvii. 29.
[7] S. xxxv. 11. [8] S. lv. 78.
[9] Sc. the Qur'ān and the Ḥadīth.
[10] *Mutashābihāt*, sc. dubious; *vid.* Massignon, *Essai*, p. 29.

Chapter VII

THEIR VARIANCE AS TO WHETHER GOD HAS CEASED CREATING

They are at variance as to whether or not God has ceased to create. The greater part of them, and the majority of their leaders and foremost men, say that it is not possible for an attribute to come to God in time which He has not had the right to claim in eternity. He did not deserve the name "Creator" because of His creating creation, or the name "Maker" because of originating mortal beings, or the name "Former" because of forming the forms: if this had been so, He would have been eternally[1] deficient, only becoming complete through the act of creation—far removed is God above that!

They hold that God is eternally the Creator, Maker, Former, Forgiving, Compassionate, Grateful, and so on, through all the attributes wherewith He has qualified Himself, being qualified by them in pre-eternity. As He is qualified by knowledge, strength, might, majesty and power, so He is similarly qualified by making (*takwīn*), shaping and forming, as well as by desire, generosity, forgiveness and gratitude. They do not differentiate between a quality which is an act, and a quality which cannot be described as an act, such as greatness, splendour, knowledge, strength. Similarly, since it is established that He is Hearing, Seeing, Powerful, Creating, Making and Forming, and that He is praised, nevertheless, if He had had the right to these names merely in virtue of the thing created, formed and made, He would have been in need of creation; and need is the sign of the temporal. Moreover, this would imply change, and the passing from one state

[1] Viz. in pre-eternity.

into another: God would have been other than Creator, and then become Creator; other than Desirous, and then become Desirous: and this would be like the "setting" which Abraham the Friend of God (peace be upon him!) denied, when he said: "I love not gods which set."[1] Creating and making are attributes of God, whereby He has been qualified pre-eternally. Now the act and the thing done are not one and the same, and so it is with shaping and making: but if the act and the thing done had been both one, then created beings would have come into being of themselves, because there would have been no relation (*ma'nā*) between God and them, except that they were not, and then were.

Some of them, however, deny the above doctrine, maintaining that it implies that creation existed along with God in pre-eternity.

They are agreed that He is without ceasing Ruler, God and Lord, without subject or slave: it is therefore in the same way permissible to say that He is Creator, Maker and Former, without any thing created, made or formed.

Chapter VIII

THEIR VARIANCE CONCERNING NAMES

They are at variance concerning the names (of God). Some of them maintain that the names of God are neither God, nor other than God: this is parallel to their doctrine concerning the attributes. Others hold the view that the names of God are God.

[1] S. vi. 76.

Chapter IX

THEIR DOCTRINE OF THE QUR'ĀN

They are agreed that the Qur'ān is the real word of God, and that it is neither created, nor originated in time, nor an innovation; that it is recited by our tongues, written in our books, and preserved in our breasts, but not dwelling therein. They are also agreed that it is neither body, nor element, nor accident.[1]

Chapter X

THEIR VARIANCE CONCERNING THE NATURE OF SPEECH

They are at variance concerning the nature of God's speech. The majority of them hold that the speech of God is an eternal attribute of God contained in His essence in no way resembling the speech of created beings; and that it possesses no quiddity (*mā'īyah*), just as His essence possesses no quiddity, except for the purpose of affirmation.[2] One of them has said: "The speech of God consists of command, prohibition, informing, promise and threat. God is eternally commanding, prohibiting, informing, promising, threatening, praising and blaming. Therefore, since ye have been created, and since your intellects are mature,[3] act

[1] Some MSS. omit this sentence and read in its place: "As God is known by our hearts, remembered by our tongues, and worshipped in our temples, without dwelling therein."

[2] Sc. God is transcendental, but also at His will immanent, for man's better instruction.

[3] Sc. ye have reached years of discretion, and are subject to the Law.

accordingly; for ye will be blamed for your disobedience, and rewarded for your obedience (and all this was already destined) when ye were created. For in the same manner we were commanded and addressed (by God) through the Qur'ān which was revealed to the Prophet, before ever we were created or came into being."

The greater part of them are agreed that God's speech does not consist of letters, sound or spelling, but that letters, sound and spelling are indications of His speech, and that they have their own instruments and members, to wit, uvula, lips and tongue. Now God has no member and needs no instrument: therefore His speech does not consist of letters or sound. One of the great Ṣūfīs said in his discourse: "Whoever speaks by means of letters is subject to cause, while he whose speech is dependent (upon some other thing) is liable to need."[1]

One sect of the Ṣūfīs holds that God's speech does consist of letters and sound, maintaining that it is only known after that fashion, and asserting that it is an attribute of God in His essence as uncreated. This is the view of Ḥārith al-Muḥāsibī, and among the moderns of Ibn Sālim.

Now the root of this matter is, that since it is established that God is pre-eternal, and that He does not resemble creation in any respect, and that His attributes likewise do not resemble the attributes of created beings, it follows that His speech does not consist of letters and sound, as does the speech of created beings. Moreover, God has asserted speech as belonging to Himself, when He says, "And Moses did God speak to, speaking";[2] and also, "We only say

[1] Speech, humanly seen, is effected through the mediumship of various bodily members, and so it is subject to cause and dependent, namely, upon the condition that these members are functioning properly. God is beyond such need.

[2] S. iv. 162.

unto a thing we wish, 'Be', and it is";[1] and again, "In order that he may hear the word of God."[2] It therefore follows of necessity that He is qualified thereby eternally: for if He had not been eternally qualified thereby, His speech would have been the speech of creatures born in time, and in pre-eternity He would have been qualified by its opposite, that is, silence or impediment; and as it is established that He does not change, and that His essence is not susceptible to events, it necessarily follows that He could not have been silent, and then found speech. Since therefore it is established that He possesses speech, and that it is not created in time, it is necessary to confess this: since on the other hand it is not established that this speech consists of letters and sound, it is necessary to withhold from such an assertion.

The word "Qur'ān" may be construed grammatically in several ways. It may be considered as the verbal noun of the stem "to recite", as where God says: "And when we recite it then follow its recitation."[3] It may also be applied to the letters of the alphabet occurring in copies of the Holy Book, as when the Prophet said: "Do not journey with the Qur'ān into the land of the enemy." The speech of God, then, is called a Qur'ān: every *qur'ān* apart from God's speech is created and originated in time, whereas the Qur'ān which is God's speech is neither created nor originated in time. The word "Qur'ān", however, is only understood in its general connotation to mean the speech of God, and in that case it is uncreated.

Those who refrain from expressing themselves on this matter do so for one of two reasons. Either they refrain because they would describe it as something created and originated in time—for it is their view that it is created—and their refraining is due to religious scruples: or they refrain because they are attached to

[1] S. xvi. 42.
[2] S. ix. 6.
[3] S. lxxv. 18.

the conception that it is an attribute of God in His essence, in which case the only explanation of their refraining from expressing and enunciating the term "creation" (as applied to this) is, that they are attached to the idea that it is an attribute of God—and God's attributes are uncreated—and so they will not be convicted of having denied what they should have affirmed. They therefore say that the Qur'ān is the speech of God, and then are silent, since neither tradition nor recited verse suggests that it is other than created: and from this standpoint they are right.

Chapter XI

THEIR DOCTRINE OF VISION

They are agreed that God will be seen with the eyes in the next world, and that the believers will see Him but not the unbelievers, because this is a grace from God: for God says, "To those who do what is good, goodness and an increase."[1] They hold that vision is possible through the intellect, and obligatory through the hearing.[2] As for its being intellectually possible, this is because God exists, and everything which exists may (logically speaking) be seen. For God has implanted in us vision: and if the vision of God had not been possible, then the petition of Moses, "O Lord, show Thyself to me, that I may look upon Thee",[3] would have been (evidence of) ignorance and unbelief. Moreover, when God made the vision dependent on the condition that the mountain should abide firm—for He says, "And if it abide firm in its place, then shalt thou see Me"[4]—and seeing also that its abiding firm

[1] S. x. 27.

[2] Sc. by deduction from the evidences in creation, and by faith in God's revelation in the Qur'ān.

[3] S. vii. 139. [4] *Ibid.*

would have been intellectually possible, if God had made it firm; it necessarily follows that the vision which was dependent on this was intellectually permissible and possible. Since therefore it is established that vision is intellectually possible, and as moreover it is shown to be obligatory through the hearing—for God says, "Faces on that day shall be bright, gazing on their Lord",[1] and again, "To those who do what is good, goodness and an increase",[2] and again, "Nay, verily, from their Lord on that day they are veiled"[3]—and as the Traditions assert that there is vision, as when the Prophet said, "Verily ye shall see your Lord as ye see the moon on the night of its fullness, without confusion in the vision of Him", concerning which matter the stories are well known and authenticated: it follows that it is necessary to state this, and to believe that it is true.

As for the esoteric interpretation of those who deny the vision of God, this is impossible, as for example those who construe "gazing on their Lord"[4] as meaning "gazing on the reward of their Lord": for the reward of God is other than God. So with those who say that "show Thyself to me, that I may look upon Thee"[5] is a petition for a sign: for God had already shown Moses His signs. It is the same with those who interpret "No vision taketh Him in"[6] as meaning that, as no vision taketh Him in in this world, so also in the world to come: God denied that He could be taken in by the vision, for such taking-in would imply modality (*kayfīyah*) and circumscription; He denied, therefore, that which implies modality and circumscription, but not the vision in which there is neither modality nor circumscription.

They are agreed that God is not seen in this world either with the eyes or with the heart, save from the point of view of faith: for this (vision) is the limit of

[1] S. lxxv. 22–3. [2] S. x. 27. [3] S. lxxxiii. 15.
[4] S. lxxv. 23. [5] S. vii. 139. [6] S. vi. 103.

grace and the noblest of blessings, and therefore cannot occur save in the noblest place.[1] If they had been vouchsafed in this world the noblest of blessings, there would have been no difference between this world which passes away, and Paradise which is eternal: and as God prevented His conversant[2] from attaining this in the present world, it is the more proper that those who are beneath him should be likewise (prevented). Moreover, this world is an abode of passing-away: therefore it is not possible for the Eternal to be seen in the abode that passes away. Further, if they[3] had seen God in this world, belief in Him would have been axiomatic (*ḍarūrah*). In short, God has stated that vision will occur in the next world, but He has not stated that it occurs in this world: and it is necessary to confine oneself to what God has expressly stated.

Chapter XII

THEIR VARIANCE AS TO THE PROPHET'S VISION

They are at variance as to whether the Prophet saw God on the night of the heavenly journey.[4] The majority of them, including the most important Ṣūfīs, declare that Muḥammad did not see Him with his eyes, nor any other created being, in this world. Moreover, it is related that 'Ā'ishah said: "Whoever asserts that Muḥammad saw his Lord, lies." This view is taken, among others, by Al-Junayd, Al-Nūrī and Abū Sa'īd

[1] Sc. Paradise.
[2] *Kalīm*, sc. Moses.
[3] Sc. the Prophets and Saints: direct vision would have robbed them of the virtue of having believed in God "in a glass, darkly".
[4] The *mi'rāj*, referred to at S. xvii. 1, and expatiated upon by the commentators.

al-Kharrāz. Certain of them, however, assert that the Prophet saw God on the night of the heavenly journey, and that he was specially designated from among men for (the grace of) vision, just as Moses was designated for (the grace of) speaking (with God). To this end they cite the story told by Ibn 'Abbās, Asmā' and Anas: and this view is supported by Abū 'Abdillāh al-Qurashī, Al-Haykal, and certain of the later Ṣūfīs. One of them has proposed that Muḥammad saw God with his heart, and not with his eyes, citing as evidence the words of God, "The heart belies not what he saw."[1]

We have not, however, known of a single shaykh of this order—that is, not one who is recognised as a valid authority—and we have not seen it stated in their books, compositions or treatises, or in the genuine stories that are related of them, neither have we heard it stated by any of those whom we have contacted, that God is seen in this world, or that any of His creation has seen Him: with the exception, that is, of a sect who have not been recognised as being of any importance among the Ṣūfīs. It is true that certain people have asserted that some of the Ṣūfīs have claimed vision: but all the shaykhs are agreed on convicting of error such as make this statement, and on refuting their claim, and they have written books to this end; among them being Abū Sa'īd al-Kharrāz; Al-Junayd has also written and discoursed much refuting and convicting of error those who make such a claim. They further assert that those who pretend to have seen God have, in reality, never known God: and these books of theirs bear witness to this fact.[2]

[1] S. liii. 11.

[2] For another discussion of this point, *vid.* Sarrāj, *Kitāb al-Luma'*, pp. 428 f., where the words of Kharrāz are quoted.

Chapter XIII

THEIR DOCTRINE OF PREDESTINATION AND THE CREATION OF ACTS

They are agreed that God is the Creator of all the acts of His servants, even as He is the Creator of their essences: that all that they do, be it good or evil, is in accordance with God's decree, predestination, desire and will; otherwise, they would not have been servants, subject to a Lord, and created. God says: "Say, God is the Creator of everything";[1] and again: "Verily, everything have we created by decree...and everything they do is in the books."[2] Now since acts are things, it necessarily follows that God is the Creator of them: for if acts had not been created, God would have been the Creator of certain things, but not of all, and then His words, "Creator of everything", would be a lie—far exalted is God above that! Moreover, it is certain that acts are more numerous than essences: therefore, if God had been the Creator of the essences, and the servants the creators of the acts, created being would have been worthier the ascription of praise for the act of creation, and the creation of the servants would have been greater than the creation of God; consequently, they would have been more perfect in power and more fruitful in creation than God. But God says: "Or have they made associates with God who can create as He creates, so that the creation seem familiar to them? Say, God is the Creator of everything, and He is the One, the Dominant."[3] So God denies that there is any creator other than Himself. God also says, "And we measured out the journey between them",[4] thereby stating that He has measured

[1] S. xiii. 17.
[2] S. liv. 49, 52.
[3] S. xiii. 17.
[4] S. xxxiv. 17.

out His servants' journey. God says further, "When God has created you and what ye make";[1] and again, "From the evil of what He has created",[2] thereby indicating that part of His creation is evil; and again, "And obey not him whose heart we have made heedless of remembrance of us",[3] that is, we created in it heedlessness; and further, "Speak ye openly or secretly, verily, He knows the nature of men's breasts! Aye! He knows who created!"[4] so stating that their speech, and all that they keep secret or expose, are His creation.

'Umar (God be well pleased with him!) said: "O Messenger of God, what thinkest thou of that in which we are engaged? Is it upon a matter which is already completed, or a matter only now begun?" The Prophet replied: "Upon a matter already completed." 'Umar said: "Then shall we not have trust?" He answered: "Perform (what ye are about), for everyone is prepared for that for which he is created." The Prophet was also asked: "What thinkest thou of the spells which we employ, and the medicine wherewith we treat ourselves? Do these reverse the decree of God?" He replied: "These come of the decree of God."[5] He also said: "Truly, no man believes, until he believes in God and in the decree of God, be it for good or for ill."

Since it is possible, then, for God to create an essence which is evil, it is also possible for Him to create an action which is evil. Now it is generally conceded that the action of a man trembling is a creation of God: it follows therefore that all other motions are the same, except that in the one case God has created both motion and freewill, and in the other motion without freewill.[6] Abū Bakr al-Wāsiṭī interpreted God's words, "His is whatsoever dwells in the night or in the day",[7] as

[1] S. xxxvii. 94.
[2] S. cxiii. 2.
[3] S. xviii. 27.
[4] S. lxvii. 13–14.
[5] For this Tradition and a discussion of it, *vid.* Nawawī's Commentary on the *Ṣaḥīḥ* of Muslim, III. pp. 90 ff. (ed. Cairo, 1347).
[6] Trembling is an *involuntary* act, and therefore without freewill.
[7] S. vi. 13.

follows: "If a man claims that anything of His kingdom—that is, 'whatsoever dwells in the night or in the day'—be it so much as a thought or a motion, is his, or through him, or for him, or from him, then he is contending with (God's) absolute authority, and weakening (His) power." As for God's words, "Aye! His is the creation and the bidding",[1] these he interprets as follows: "'Creation' is bringing into being, and 'bidding' is setting at liberty: if God had not bidden the limbs with a bidding of setting at liberty, they could not have accorded with Him in any matter, nor likewise could they have opposed Him."

Chapter XIV

THEIR DOCTRINE OF CAPACITY

They are agreed that every breath they draw, every glance they make, and every motion they perform, is by virtue of a faculty which God originates in them, and a capacity which He creates for them at the same time as their actions, neither before them nor after them, and that no action can be performed without these: for otherwise they would have the attribute of God, doing whatever they wished, and decreeing whatever they desired, and God would no longer be the Strong, the Powerful—in His words, "And God does what He wishes"[2]—any more than any poor, weak, contemptible slave.

If this capacity had consisted in the possession of healthy limbs, every person so endowed would be of equal attainment: but experience shows that a man may possess healthy limbs, but his actions may not be similarly sound. It follows, then, that capacity does not derive from faculty and express itself in healthy limbs:

[1] S. vii. 52. [2] S. iii. 35.

faculty is a thing which varies in degree at various times, as any man may observe with regard to himself. Moreover, since faculty is an accident, and accident cannot persist of itself, or through anything persisting in it—for if a thing does not exist of itself, and if nothing else exists through it, it cannot persist through the persistence of any other thing, because the persistence of something else does not connote persistence for it—it follows that that thing cannot have any persistence in itself:[1] and this being so, the inevitable conclusion is that the faculty of each single action is different from the faculty of any other action.[2] Had the case been otherwise, men would have had no need or necessity of recourse to God at the time of their actions, and God's words, "And to Thee we pray for help",[3] would be meaningless. Further, if the faculty had existed before the act, and not persisted up to the time of the act, the act would have been performed with a nullified faculty, that is, without any faculty whatsoever: which implies abolishing the relationship of Lord and servant altogether. For if this had been the case, it would have been possible for an act to occur without faculties, that is, it would have been possible for acts to exist of themselves, without any agent. But God says, in the story of Moses and the upright servant, "Verily, thou canst never have patience with me";[4] and when He says, "That is the interpretation of what thou couldst not have patience with",[5] He means, "what thou hast not the faculty to do".

They are agreed that they are accredited with acts and merit[6] in a true sense, for which they are rewarded and punished, and on account of which God issued command and prohibition, and announced promises

[1] The subject changes.

[2] K. argues to the position that God intervenes in every act, so escaping from a rigid fatalism.

[3] S. i. 4. [4] S. xviii. 66. [5] S. xviii. 81.

[6] *iktisāb*, personal responsibility.

and threats: the meaning of the term "merit" being, that a man acts through a faculty (divinely) originated. A certain Ṣūfī said: "The meaning of 'merit' is, that a man acts in order to acquire a benefit or repel a disadvantage": so God says, "It shall have what it has earned, and it shall owe what has been earned from it."[1] They are further agreed that they exercise freewill and desire with respect to their "merit", and that they are not constrained or forced into it against their will. We mean by "freewill" that God has created in us freewill, and therefore there is no question of compulsion in these matters or of renunciation.[2] Al-Ḥasan ibn 'Alī said: "God is not obeyed through compulsion, nor is He disobeyed by reason of an overwhelming force: He has not left His servant entirely without work to do in (His) kingdom." Sahl ibn 'Abdillāh said: "God did not strengthen the pious through compulsion, He strengthened them through faith."[3] One of the great Ṣūfīs said: "Whoever believes not in predestination is an infidel, and whoever says that it is impossible to disobey God is a sinner."[4]

Chapter XV

THEIR DOCTRINE OF COMPULSION

Some of them have declared the idea of compulsion to be absurd, saying that compulsion can only occur in the case of two persons being unyielding, that is to say, when one person gives an order to another, and the other refuses (to obey), and then the former compels the latter to (do) so. The meaning of compulsion

[1] S. ii. 286.
[2] *tafwīḍ*, committing everything to God: cf. S. xl. 47.
[3] Thus securing merit for them.
[4] For predestination, as previously shown, does not negative freewill.

is, that the agent should be constrained to do a certain thing, although he dislikes it and prefers something else, so that he then chooses to perform that which he dislikes, and leaves alone that which he likes: but for this constraint and compulsion, he would certainly have done the thing which he has left alone, and left alone the thing which he has done. Now we find nothing of this sort in the matter of men's acquiring[1] faith or unbelief, obedience or disobedience. The believer chooses belief, likes it, approves of it, desires it, and prefers it to its opposite; while he dislikes unbelief, hates it, disapproves of it, does not desire it, and prefers its opposite to it. God has created for him the choice, approval and desire for faith, and the hatred, dislike and disapproval for disbelief: for God says, "God has made faith beloved by you, and has made it seemly in your hearts, and has made misbelief and iniquity and rebellion hateful to you."[2] The unbeliever, on the other hand, chooses unbelief, approves of it, likes it, desires it, and prefers it to its opposite; while he dislikes belief, hates it, disapproves of it, does not desire it, and prefers its opposite to it. God has created all this: for He says, "So do we make seemly to every nation their work";[3] and again, "But whomsoever He wishes to lead astray, He makes his breast tight and straight."[4] Neither of them was prevented from (following) the opposite of what he chose, or forced into that which he acquired: therefore they are all bound by God's proof and subject to His pronouncement. The resort of unbelievers is hell for what they have earned,[5] and "We have not wronged them, but it was themselves they wronged".[6] God does what He wills,[7] "He shall not be questioned concerning what He does, but they shall be questioned."[8]

[1] *iktisāb.*
[2] S. xlix. 7.
[3] S. vi. 107.
[4] S. vi. 125.
[5] S. ix. 96 (cf.).
[6] S. xliii. 76.
[7] S. ii. 254, etc. (cf.).
[8] S. xxi. 23.

Ibn al-Farghānī said: "There is neither thought nor motion, save by the command of God. This is the meaning of God's word, 'Be!';[1] for His is the creation of the command, and the command of the creation,[2] and creation is His attribute. By these two letters[3] He left no room for any intelligent man to claim that anything in this world or the next is either his, or through him, or for him. Know, therefore, that there is no god save God!"

Chapter XVI

THEIR DOCTRINE OF ADVANTAGEOUSNESS

They are agreed that God does with His servants whatever He wishes, and decrees for them however He desires, whether that be to their advantage or not: for the creation is His creation, and the command is His command[4]—"He shall not be questioned concerning what He does, but they shall be questioned."[5] But for this, there would have been no difference between servant and Lord. God says, "Let not those who misbelieve reckon that our letting them range is good for themselves. We only let them have their range that they may increase in sin";[6] and again, "God only wishes to torment them therewith in the life of this world, and that their souls may pass away while still they misbelieve";[7] and again, "These are they whose hearts God wished not to purify."[8] The doctrine of "the greatest advantage" implies that (God's) power is limited, and that His treasuries are not inexhaustible, and that God Himself is in such respect incapable: for if He has dealt with men to the "limit of their advan-

[1] S. ii. 111, etc. (cf.). [2] S. vii. 52 (cf.)
[3] Sc. *kāf* and *nūn*, the letters forming the word *kun*.
[4] S. vii. 52 (cf.). [5] S. xxi. 23. [6] S. iii. 172.
[7] S. ix. 55. [8] S. v. 45.

tage", there remains nothing beyond that "limit", so that if God even wished to augment their "advantage", He would be unable to do so, and would not find any means to grant them any further "advantage" beyond what He had already given them—God is far removed above this!

They are agreed that all God's dealings with His servants—kindness, health, security, faith, guidance, favour—are only a condescension on His part: if He had not acted thus, it would still have been quite feasible. This is in no way incumbent upon God: for if God had been obliged to follow any such course of action, He would not have been deserving of praise and gratitude.

They are agreed that reward and punishment are not a question of merit, but of God's will, generosity and justice: men do not deserve eternal punishment on account of sins from which they have afterwards desisted, neither do they deserve an eternal and unlimited reward because of a limited number of (good) deeds.

They are agreed that if God should punish all who dwell in heaven and earth, He would not be unjust to them, and that if He should bring every unbeliever into Paradise, it would not be an impossible thing: for creation is His creation, and command is His command.[1] But He has stated that He will bless believers eternally, and punish unbelievers eternally, and He is true in what He says, and what He states is the truth. Therefore He is obliged to deal with men thus, and it is not possible for Him to do otherwise: for God does not lie therein—God is far removed above this!

They are agreed that God does not do things for any cause: for if they had a cause, then that cause would have a cause, and so *ad infinitum*; and that is false. God says, "Verily, those for whom the better portion from us was foreordained, they from it shall be kept far away";[2] and again, "He has elected you";[3] and again,

[1] S. vii. 52 (cf.). [2] S. xxi. 101. [3] S. xxii. 77.

"And the word of thy Lord is fulfilled, 'I will surely fill hell with jinn and mankind altogether'";[1] and again, "We have created for hell many of the jinn and mankind."[2] Naught of this is unjust or wrong: for injustice is a thing forbidden, and really consists of putting a thing out of its place;[3] while wrong is a swerving from the path that has been set forth, and the ideal which has been set up by Him Who is above, and beneath Whose power all men are. Since God is not beneath the power of any person, and since He has no commander or chider above Him, He cannot be unjust in what He does, or wrong in aught that He decrees. There is nothing foul in Him: for foul is what He has made foul, and fair what He has made fair. A certain man said: "Foul is what He has forbidden, and fair what He has commanded." Muḥammad ibn Mūsā said: "Fair-seeming things are fair through His revelation, and foul-seeming things foul through His veiling: these are two attributes which persist in post-eternity as they have persisted in pre-eternity." This means, that what restores thee to God from things is fair, and what restores thee to things and not to Him is foul: so that foul and fair are things whose natures God has prescribed in pre-eternity. Or else it may mean that what seems fair is revealed[4] from the veil of prohibition, so that there is no veil between man and it; while foul is behind the veil, that is, the prohibition. The latter interpretation conforms with the saying of Muḥammad: "And over the gates are trailing veils"; it is said that the open gates are God's inviolable ordinances (*maḥārim*), while the veils are His interdictions (*ḥudūd*).

[1] S. xi. 120. [2] S. vii. 178.

[3] Under some circumstances, stern measures must be taken, as against gross offenders; but to be ruthless under all circumstances would be unjust.

[4] Reading *tajallī* with the MSS., cf. "through His revelation" above. I was persuaded by the native printer against my will to change this reading to *takhallī*.

Chapter XVII

THEIR DOCTRINE OF PROMISE AND THREAT

They are agreed that the absolute threat (of God) applies to unbelievers, and the absolute promise to those who perform good works. Some have maintained that remission of minor sins is secured by the avoidance of major sins, for God says: "If ye avoid great sins from which ye are forbidden," etc.[1] Others put them in the same category as major sins as regards the possibility of punishment, adducing the divine authority, "If ye show what is in your souls, or hide it, God will call you to account."[2] They explain the words, "If ye avoid great sins from which ye are forbidden", as referring to polytheism and infidelity: it[3] includes many species, which may be considered as being covered by the plural noun.[4] Another interpretation is, however, possible, namely, that the sentence refers to a number of persons, each one of whom is guilty of a major *sin*, so that collectively they are called major *sins*.

They make the possibility of the remission of major sins to depend on the (divine) will and the (Prophet's) intercession. They hold that it is necessary and certain that the people of prayer[5] will be delivered from hell because of their faith: for God says, "Verily, God pardons not associating aught with Him, but He pardons anything short of that to whomsoever He pleases",[6] thus making (His) will a condition in respect of (forgiving) what is less than polytheism.

Briefly, they hold that the believer is between fear and hope: he hopes for God's generosity in the re-

[1] S. iv. 35. [2] S. ii. 284.
[3] Sc. *kafr*, the great sin *par excellence*.
[4] Sc. *kabā'ir*. [5] Muslims. [6] S. iv. 51.

mission of major sins, and fears His punishment of minor sins; for forgiveness is implicit in (God's) will, and (God's) will is not conditioned by any consideration of major or minor sin. Those who lay down strict and severe conditions for repentance, and the commission of minor sins, do not thereby intend to imply that (God's) threat is a necessary consequence, but rather to magnify the seriousness of the sin by emphasising what is consequently due to God, in order to secure abstention from committing what God has forbidden. They only use the term "minor sin" relatively, as comparing one sin with another. They demand of every soul that it shall pay in full what is due to God, and that it shall abstain from what God has forbidden, and perform in full what God has commanded, having in view what shortcomings attach to the conditions of any act. With all this, they are the most hopeful of men as to what concerns others, but the most fearful as to what concerns themselves: it would even seem that God's threats only apply to them, while His promises are only for others. Al-Fuḍayl was asked, on the evening of 'Arafah,[1] "What thinkest thou of the state of mankind?" He replied: "Forgiven, but for my presence among them." Sarī al-Saqaṭī said: "I look into the glass many times a day, fearing lest my face may have turned black."[2] He also said: "I do not wish to die where I am known, for I fear that the earth would not receive me, and I should be a thing exposed." They also have of all men the fairest thoughts of their Lord. Yaḥyā said: "If a man has not a fair thought of God, he does not rejoice in God." But of themselves they have the worst thoughts of all men, and the meanest consideration, not accounting themselves worthy of any good, whether of this world or the other.

[1] The 9th day of Dhu 'l-Ḥijjah.

[2] As will happen to unbelievers on the Last Day: *vid.* S. iii. 103. The faces of believers, however, will be whitened.

In short, God says, "And others have confessed their sins, that they have mixed with a righteous action another evil one",[1] so laying down that the believer has two (kinds of) acts, one righteous, the other evil: the righteous counts for him, the evil against him. God has promised reward for the deed which is for him, and threatened punishment for the deed which is against him: the threat is what is owing to God from His servants, and the promise is what is owing to the servants from God—that is, in so far as God has imposed it upon Himself as an obligation. If He exacted from them the full payment of His dues, and did not (in return) pay them their dues in full, that would not be in keeping with His generosity, seeing that He is independent of them, whereas they are dependent on Him: but it is more consonant with His generosity, and more in accord with His goodness, that He should pay them their dues, and even more than their dues—so generous is He—and Himself discharge the debt which they owe Him. So God declares, "Verily, God would not wrong by the weight of an atom; and if it is a good work, He will double it and bring from Himself a mighty hire":[2] the words "from Himself" imply that this is an act of condescension, and not in any way a reward.

Chapter XVIII

THEIR DOCTRINE OF INTERCESSION

They are agreed upon confirming all that God has mentioned in His Book about intercession, and all that has come down in the stories told of the Prophet. God says, "And in the end thy Lord will give thee, and thou shalt be well pleased";[3] "It may be that thy Lord

[1] S. ix. 103. [2] S. iv. 42. [3] S. xciii. 5.

will raise thee to a laudable station";[1] "And they shall not intercede except for him with whom He is pleased";[2] and the infidels say, "But we have no intercessors".[3] The Prophet said: "My intercession is over those of my community who have committed major sins." He also said: "My prayer conceals intercession for my community."

They believe in the Path,[4] holding that it is a bridge stretched over hell. Once 'Ā'ishah recited the words "On the day when the earth shall be changed for another earth",[5] and then asked, "Where will mankind be then, O Messenger of God?" The Prophet replied: "On the Path."

They believe in the Balance, holding that the deeds of men will be weighed, as God says: "And whosesoever scales are heavy, they are prosperous; but whosesoever scales are light...."[6] This they believe, even though they do not know how the matter will be accomplished: for of this, and of like matters the manner of whose accomplishment they do not understand, they say, "We believe in what God has said, according to what God thereby intended, and we believe in what God's Messenger has said, according to what he intended."

They believe that God will deliver from hell every man in whose heart there is an atom's weight of faith, in accordance with the tradition.[7] They believe that heaven and hell are eternal, but created, enduring for ever and ever without passing away or being destroyed; and similarly that their inhabitants continue in them eternally, blessed or punished for ever, with a bliss that never ends, or a punishment that never ceases.

In their outward affairs they attest their faith before

[1] S. xvii. 81. [2] S. xxi. 28–9. [3] S. xxvi. 100.

[4] Sc. the bridge of A'rāf, mentioned in S. vii. 44, over which all men will pass to Judgment.

[5] S. xiv. 49. [6] S. vii. 7.

[7] In its usual form, "a mustard-grain of faith": *vid.* Wensinck, *Concordance*, p. 111.

the community of believers, but their inward hearts they entrust to God. They believe that the Abode is an abode of faith and resignation,[1] and that its inhabitants are believers and Muslims. According to their view, those Muslims who commit major sins are believers by virtue of the faith which they possess, but evil-doers because of the corruption which is in them. They hold that it is right to pray behind any (Imām), whether he be a man of piety or a sinner. They also hold that it is right to pray for every person who dies, provided he be one of those to turn to Mecca.[2] They hold that the observance of Friday, and the assemblies (of Muslims), and feasts, is binding upon every Muslim who has no legitimate excuse, under the leadership of any Imām, be he pious or sinful; and likewise the Holy War and the Pilgrimage. They hold that the Caliphate is true, and that it resides in the house of Quraysh. They are agreed on the precedence of Abū Bakr, ʿUmar, ʿUthmān and ʿAlī. They hold that it is right to imitate the Companions and the holy men of old, but are silent as to the disputes which existed between them, holding, however, that these in no way detracted from the "better portion" foreordained to them by God.

They believe that every man concerning whom the Prophet testified that he would enter Paradise is in fact in Paradise, and that such a man will not be punished in hell. They hold that it is not right to take the sword against governors, even though they commit wrong. They hold that it is the duty of all, so far as they are able, to do good, and to refrain from doing evil, with kindness, mercy, considerateness, compassion, goodness, and gentleness of speech. They believe in the punishment of the grave, and the inquisition of Munkar and Nakīr.[3] They believe in the ascension of the

[1] Sc. Islam, as opposed to the "Abode of War", or heathendom.

[2] Lit. "the people of *qiblah*".

[3] The angels who question man in the grave: cf. S. xlvii. 29 and the commentators thereon.

Prophet, and that he was carried to the seventh heaven,[1] and to whatever God willed, in a single night, while waking, in the flesh. They attest the veracity of visions, holding that they are tidings of good cheer to believers, or warning, to give them pause. Lastly, they maintain that when a man dies, or is slain, it is in the fullness of his destiny: they do not agree that a man's destiny can be thought of as falling suddenly,[2] but hold that when it comes, it comes at its proper time, and cannot be put back or forward a single hour.

Chapter XIX

THEIR DOCTRINE OF CHILDREN

They believe that the children of believers are with their parents in Paradise: but concerning the children of unbelievers they are at variance. Some teach that God punishes no man with hell, save he be fully convicted of rebellion and unbelief, so that he has fallen under the judgment. The majority refer[3] their affairs to God, holding that it is open to God either to punish or to bless them. They are agreed that it is right to moisten the shoes.[4] They hold that it is possible that God may give to eat what is unlawful.[5] They dis-

[1] On the night of the Heavenly Journey, referred to at S. xvii. 1. The traditionists expand the very meagre reference given there, and differ as to the details, some holding that the Prophet was raised to the sixth, some to the seventh heaven. *Vid.* Nawawī's commentary on the *Ṣaḥīḥ* of Muslim, III, pp. 4 ff.

[2] The word *ikhtirām* is used of death overtaking a person suddenly and unexpectedly. K. points out that, as every man's destiny is already fore-ordained, death cannot be regarded as a thing which happens unexpectedly.

[3] The verb *arja'a* is used, recalling the views of the Murji'ites.

[4] As a part of ablution (*wuḍū'*): *vid.* Wensinck, *Handbook*, p. 262.

[5] Contrary to the doctrine of the Mu'tazilites, as Qōnawī points out in his commentary on this passage.

approve of (all) quarrelling and disputing about religion, and animosity and hostility concerning predestination, holding that it is better to be occupied with what is in store for one,[1] rather than to indulge in animosities over religion.

They hold that the quest for knowledge is the noblest of acts, meaning thereby the knowledge of the appointed time,[2] and the outward and inward duties which it imposes. They are the most kindly of men towards God's creatures, making no distinction between Arab (*faṣīḥ*) and foreigner (*'ajam*), and the most generous in giving of what they own, but the most careful in abstaining from what others possess, and the most sincere in turning from this world, being the most anxious to follow the Sunnah and the practices of the saints,[3] and the most jealous in pursuing them.

Chapter XX

THEIR DOCTRINE OF THE DUTIES IMPOSED BY GOD ON ADULTS

They are agreed that all the ordinances imposed by God on (His) servants in His Book, and all the duties laid down by the Prophet (in the Traditions), are a necessary obligation and a binding imposition for adults of mature intelligence: and that they may not be abandoned or forsaken in any way by any man, whether he be a veracious believer (*ṣiddīq*), or a saint, or a gnostic, even though he may have attained the furthest rank, the highest degree, the noblest station,

[1] Lit. "what is for and against", i.e. in the assessment of the acts.

[2] The prescribed time for performing religious duties: there is no need to suppose that the word here carries the special mystical significance attached to it by the Ṣūfīs.

[3] *āthār*.

or the most exalted stage. They hold that there is no station in which a man may dispense with the prescriptions (*ādāb*) of the religious law, by holding permissible what God has prohibited, or making illegal what God has declared legal, or legal what God has pronounced illegal, or omitting to perform any religious duty without due excuse or reason, which excuse and reason are defined by the agreed judgment of all Muslims and approved by the prescriptions of the religious law. The more inwardly pure a man is, the higher his rank and the nobler his station, so much the more arduously he labours, with sincerer performance and a greater fear (of God).

They are agreed that acts are not a cause of happiness or unhappiness, but that happiness and unhappiness are predestined and prescribed by the will of God: so runs the Tradition, on the authority of ʿAbdullāh ibn ʿUmar, that the Prophet said, "This is a book from the Lord of the Worlds, and in it are the names of the people of Paradise, together with the names of their parents and tribes"; then the sum total is made up to the last name, and thereafter there will be no increase or decrease in their numbers ever. In the same manner the Prophet spoke of the people of hell, saying: "The happy man is he who was happy in his mother's womb, and the unhappy man he who was unhappy in his mother's womb."[1] They are further agreed that acts do not determine reward or punishment in consideration of merit, but that reward and punishment accord with God's bounty and justice, and God's determination. They are agreed that the bliss of Paradise belongs to those to whom happiness[2] has been foreordained by God, without any cause, and that the punishment of hell belongs to those to whom unhappiness has been foreordained by God, without any cause: so the Tradition runs, "These are in Paradise, and I do not care,

[1] Sc. before he came into this world.
[2] Some MSS. read "the better portion".

and these are in hell, and I do not care." God says, "We have created for hell many of the jinn and mankind";[1] and again, "Verily, those for whom the better portion from us was foreordained, they from it shall be kept far away."[2] They say that men's deeds are marks and signs of what has been foreordained for them by God,[3] as the Prophet said: "Act, for everyone is prepared for that for which he was created." Al-Junayd said: "Obedience swiftly brings glad tidings according to what God has foreordained for the obedient, and similarly with disobedience." Another Ṣūfī said: "Acts of worship are an adornment to the outward parts, and when a man adorns his limbs, God does not permit him to leave them unoccupied."[4] Muḥammad ibn 'Alī al-Kattānī said: "Acts are the raiment of servanthood: those whom God put far (from Him) at the allotment (of destinies) strip off this raiment, but those whom God drew near (to Him) admire it and cleave to it."

Nevertheless, they are agreed that God rewards and punishes for the acts: for He promised on account of righteous deeds, and threatened in connection with evil deeds; and He fulfils His promise and realises His threat, for He is true, and what He says is the truth. They say that it is the duty of every man to strive his utmost to perform what has been prescribed for him to do, and to discharge what he has been called upon to do subsequent to that prescription: and when he has fully discharged his duty, then follow the revelations, in accordance with the Tradition: "If a man acts in accordance with what he knows, God will bequeath him the knowledge of what he does not know." God says, "But those who fight strenuously for us we will surely guide them into our way";[5] and again, "O ye

[1] S. vii. 178.
[2] S. xxi. 101.
[3] Because it is then possible to see whether a man is destined for heaven or hell.
[4] Sc. with acts of worship.
[5] S. xxix. 69.

who believe! fear God and crave the means to approach Him, and be strenuous in His way, haply ye will prosper then."[1] Yaḥyā said: "The spirit of gnosis will never reach thy heart, so long as there is a duty owing to Him which thou hast not discharged." Al-Junayd said: "God will deal with His servants at the last after the manner in which He dealt with them at the first. He originated them with honour, commanded them with compassion, and promised them with condescension, and he will give them increase with honour. If a man beholds His ancient goodness, it will be easy for him to discharge His command; and if he follows out His command, he will obtain His promise; and if he possesses His promise, there is no doubt that He will give him increase." Sahl ibn 'Abdillāh al-Tustarī said: "If a man closes his eyes to God but the twinkling of an eye, he will not be guided for the length of his life."

Chapter XXI

THEIR DOCTRINE OF THE GNOSIS OF GOD

They are agreed that the only guide to God is God Himself, holding that the function of the intellect is the function of an intelligent person who is in need of a guide: for the intellect is a thing originated in time, and as such only serves as a guide to things like itself.[2] A certain man said to Al-Nūrī: "What is the guide to God?" He replied: "God." The other asked: "Then what of the intellect?" Al-Nūrī said: "The intellect is weak, and that which is weak only guides to what is weak like itself." Ibn 'Aṭā said: "The intellect is an instrument of servanthood, not a means of

[1] S. v. 39.

[2] As against the view of the Mu'tazilites, who held that God could be known through the intellect.

approaching lordship."[1] Another said: "The intellect goes about creation (*kawn*), but when it beholds the creator (*mukawwin*) it dissolves." Al-Qaḥṭabī said: "That which is comprised by the intellects is subject (to them), save from the point of view of postulation: if God had not made Himself known to the intellects by His kindnesses, they would not have attained Him even to the point of postulation."[2] They quote the following verses written by a great Ṣūfī:[3]

> Whoso seeks God, and takes the intellect for guide,
> God drives him forth, in vain distraction to abide;
> With wild confusion He confounds his inmost heart,
> So that, distraught, he cries, "I know not if Thou art."

A great Ṣūfī has said: "None knows Him, save him to whom He has made Himself known; none declares His unity, save him to whom He has declared that He is One; none believes in Him, save him to whom He has shown bounty; none describes Him, save him to whose conscience He has revealed Himself; none is true to Him, save him whom He has drawn to Himself; none is righteous towards Him, save him whom He has chosen for Himself." By "him to whom He has made Himself known" he means "him to whom God has made Himself known", and by "him to whom He has declared that He is One" he means "He has shown him that He is One." Al-Junayd said: "Gnosis is of two sorts: gnosis of Self-revelation (*ta'arruf*), and gnosis of instruction (*ta'rīf*)." The meaning of "Self-revelation" is, that He causes them to know Him, and to know things through Him, or, in the words of Abraham, "I love not gods that set":[4] the meaning of "instruction" is, that He shows them the effects of His power in the heavens and in the souls, and then

[1] Sc. it is sufficient for guiding the acts which man, as servant, must perform for God, but not as a guide to God.

[2] The intellect only makes the postulate that God is, because of God's own revelation.

[3] Sc. Ḥallāj.

[4] S. vi. 76.

implants in them a special grace (*luṭf*), so that the (material) things indicate that there is a Maker. This is the gnosis of the main body of believers, while the former is the gnosis of the elect: and no man has known God in reality, save through God. So Muḥammad ibn Wāsiʿ said: "I never saw a single thing, without seeing God in it." Another Ṣūfī said: "I never saw a single thing without seeing God before it." Ibn ʿAṭā said: "God has revealed Himself to the commoners through His creation, for He says, 'Do they not look at the camel, how she is created?'[1] To the elect He has revealed Himself through His speech and attributes, for He says, 'Do they not meditate on the Qur'ān?';[2] and again, 'And we will send down of the Qur'ān that which is a healing and a mercy to the believers',[3] 'but God's are the good names'.[4] To the prophets He has revealed Himself through Himself, for He says, 'And thus we have inspired thee by a spirit at our bidding';[5] and again, 'Hast thou not looked to thy Lord, how He prolongs the shadow?'"[6] One of the great gnostics composed the following verses:[7]

Now stands no more between the Truth and me
    Or reasoned demonstration,
    Or proof, or revelation:
Now, brightly blazing forth, Truth's luminary
    Hath driven out of sight
    Each flickering, lesser light.

He only knoweth God, whom God hath shown
    Himself: shall the eternal
    Be known of the diurnal?
Not in his handiwork may God be known:
    Can endless time be pent
    Into a chance event?

Of Him, through Him, and unto Him, a sign
    Of truth, an attestation
    He grants through inspiration:[8]

[1] S. lxxxviii. 17. [2] S. iv. 84. [3] S. xvii. 84.
[4] S. vii. 179. [5] S. xlii. 52. [6] S. xxv. 47.
[7] These verses by Ḥallāj are printed in Massignon's *Textes Hallajiens*, p. 13, with some omissions. [8] Sc. the Qur'ān.

Of Him, through Him, His own, a truth divine,
A knowledge proved and sure
Hath made our hearts secure.

This I have proven, this I now declare,
This is my faith unbending,
And this my joy unending:
There is no god but God! no rivals share
His peerless majesty,
His claimed supremacy.[1]

When men have been alone with God, and know,
This is their tongues' expression,
And this their hearts' confession:
This ecstasy of joy knits friend and foe
In common brotherhood,
Working to common good.

One of the great Ṣūfīs said: "God made us to know Himself through Himself, and guided us to the knowledge of Himself through Himself, so that the attestation of gnosis arose out of gnosis through gnosis, after he who possessed gnosis had been taught gnosis by Him Who is the object of gnosis." This means, that there is no cause of gnosis, except that God teaches gnosis to the gnostic, who therefore knows Him through His teaching him. One of the great Shaykhs said: "Any manifestation of material objects (*mukawwanāt*) may be known as such by the intellect bursting in upon it. God is too great for the intellects to burst in upon Him: He Himself taught us that He is our Lord; for He said, 'Am I not your Lord?'[2] not, 'Who am I?' thereby giving scope to the intellects to burst in upon Him; this when He first appeared as their teacher.[3] Therefore He is independent of the intellects and exalted above the perceptions."

They are agreed that no man knows God, save he possess an intellect, for the intellect is the instrument by means of which man knows whatever he may know: nevertheless, he cannot know God of himself. Abū

[1] I have expanded a little to make the sense clearer.
[2] S. vii. 171.
[3] On the day of creation.

Bakr al-Sabbāk said: "When God created the intellect, He said to it, 'Who am I?' It was silent: so He anointed[1] it with the light of Oneness (*waḥdānīyah*); and it opened its eyes, and said, 'Thou art God; there is no god except Thee'." The intellect, then, had not the capacity to know God, except through God.

Chapter XXII

THEIR VARIANCE AS TO THE NATURE OF GNOSIS

They are at variance as to the nature of gnosis itself. Al-Junayd said: "Gnosis is the realisation of thy ignorance when His knowledge comes." A bystander said: "Tell us more." He continued: "He is at once the subject and object of gnosis."[2] By these words he means that "thou art ignorant of Him in the aspect of thouness, and only attainest gnosis of Him through the aspect of Heness".[3] This is like the saying of Sahl: "Gnosis is the gnosis of ignorance." Sahl also said: "Knowledge is established by gnosis, and the intellect is established by knowledge, but as for gnosis, it is established by its own essence." This means, that when God causes a man to have gnosis of Himself, so that he knows God through His Self-revelation to him, He then originates in him a knowledge: that man therefore attains knowledge through gnosis, and intellect works in him upon the knowledge which God originated in him. Another Ṣūfī said: "The examination of the outward aspect of things is knowledge, and the examination of them with the revelation of their

[1] Lit. "smeared with kohl".
[2] God is *'ārif* and *ma'rūf*.
[3] A commonplace with the Ṣūfīs: "thou" implies multiplicity, while "He" indicates that all "otherness" is swallowed up in God.

inward aspects is gnosis." Another said: "God has made knowledge free to all believers, but gnosis He has reserved for His saints." Abū Bakr al-Warrāq said: "Gnosis is the gnosis of things in their forms and names, but knowledge is the knowledge of things in their realities."[1] Abū Sa'īd al-Kharrāz said: "The gnosis of God is the knowledge of the quest for God, before the actual experience of Him: the knowledge of God is after the experience. Therefore the knowledge of God is more secret and subtler than the gnosis of God." Fāris said: "Gnosis absorbs (the gnostic) in the essence of the Object of his gnosis." Another Ṣūfī said: "Gnosis consists of despising all values save God's, and of seeing no other value beside God's." A man asked Dhu 'l-Nūn: "By what means didst thou attain gnosis of thy Lord?" He replied: "If ever I intended an act of disobedience, and then recalled the glory of God, I was ashamed before Him." This means that he took his awareness of God's nearness as a proof of the gnosis of God. A man said to 'Ulayyān: "How art thou with regard to the Lord?" He replied: "I have not turned away from Him since the day I knew Him." The other said: "Since when hast thou known Him?" He answered: "Since the day they called me mad (*majnūn*)." Hereby he took his reverence for God's power as a proof of his gnosis of God. Sahl said: "Glory be to Him, of Whose gnosis men have attained naught but (the knowledge) that they are incapable of knowing Him."

[1] This and the following put forward the less common view, that *'ilm* is superior to *ma'rifah*: cf. Massignon, *Passion*, p. 777.

Chapter XXIII

THEIR DOCTRINE OF SPIRIT

Al-Junayd said: "The spirit (*rūḥ*) is a thing the knowledge of which God has reserved to Himself, not suffering any of His creatures to understand it. Therefore, it cannot be expressed in any other way than as being existent (*mawjūd*). God says: 'Say: The spirit is of the bidding of my Lord'."[1] Abū 'Abdillāh al-Nibājī said: "The spirit is a body which is too subtle to be perceived, and too great to be touched: it cannot be expressed in any other way than as being existent." Ibn 'Aṭā said: "God created the spirits before the bodies: for He says, 'And we created you', that is, the spirits, 'then we formed you',[2] that is, the bodies." Another Ṣūfī said: "The spirit is a subtle (essence) materialising in a dense (body), just as sight, which is a subtle essence, materialises in a dense (body)."

The majority are agreed that the spirit is an object[3] through which the body lives. One Ṣūfī said: "It is a light, fragrant breath (*rūḥ*) through which life subsists, while the soul (*nafs*) is a hot wind (*rīḥ*) through which the motions and desires exist." Al-Qaḥṭabī said: "It never entered under the humiliation of 'Be'"—this in answer to the question, What is the spirit? In his view, then, its only function is to produce life: and being alive, as well as producing life, is the attribute of Him Who causes life, just as shaping and creating are an attribute of the Creator.[4] This view he bases on the words of God: "Say: The spirit is of the command of my Lord." They interpret "command"

[1] S. xvii. 88. [2] S. vii. 10.

[3] *ma'nā*, which the Commentator is at pains to explain as not meaning "attribute" here, but *shay'*.

[4] That is, the spirit is divine, and was not created by the fiat *Kun* on the day of creation.

here as meaning God's speech, and His speech is not created: but this is as much as to say that whatever possesses life only came to life through God saying "Be alive", so that the spirit in that case is not a thing (existing) in the body at all.[1]

Chapter XXIV

THEIR DOCTRINE OF ANGELS AND MESSENGERS

The majority of the Ṣūfīs refrain from entering into the question whether the Messengers[2] are to be preferred above the Angels, or *vice versa*, saying that superiority belongs to those whom God has preferred, and that it is a matter of neither essence nor act.[3] Some, however, prefer the messengers, and some the angels. Muḥammad ibn al-Faḍl said: "The whole body of angels is more excellent than the whole body of believers, but there are certain ones among the believers who are more excellent than the angels." This is as much as to say that the prophets are more excellent.

They are agreed that certain of the messengers are more excellent than others, citing God's words: "We did prefer some of the prophets over others."[4] They refuse, however, to specify which of them is preferred, and which not, thereby agreeing with the behest of the Prophet: "Do not choose between the prophets." Nevertheless, they lay it down as a principle that Muḥammad is the most excellent of all the prophets,

[1] This seems a deliberate misunderstanding of the intention of Qaḥṭabī, which is obviously tinged with *ḥulūl*: some MSS. add, "This is not a sound view: the sound view is, that the spirit is something dwelling in the body, created like the body."

[2] Sc. the Prophets.

[3] I.e. not dependent on the personal qualities, but on God's dispensation.

[4] S. xvii. 57.

basing their doctrine on his saying, "I am the lord of the sons of Adam, without boasting: Adam and all after him are beneath my banner", and other of his sayings; as well as on the words of God, "Ye were the best of communities brought forth unto man"[1]—for since they were the best of communities, and they were his community, it follows that their prophet was the best of prophets—this, and the other proofs of his pre-eminence which are to be found in the Qur'ān.

They are all agreed that the prophets are more excellent than men, and that there is no man who can contest with the prophets in excellence, be he true believer, saint, or any other, however great his power and mighty his position. The Prophet said to 'Alī: "These twain are the lords of the elders of the people of Paradise, both former and latter, save only the prophets and messengers", referring in these words to Abū Bakr and 'Umar, and implying that they are the best of mankind after the prophets. Abū Yazīd al-Bisṭāmī said: "The final end of true believers is the first state of the prophets, and the end of the prophets has no attainable goal." Sahl ibn 'Abdillāh said: "The purposes of the gnostics reach as far as the veil, and they there halt with glance cast down: then leave is given them, and they make greeting; and they are clothed with the robe of divine strength, and are assigned exemption from error. The purposes of the prophets, however, move around the Throne, and are clothed with lights: their values are exalted, and they are joined with the Almighty; and He causes their personal ambitions to pass away, and strips off their quality of desire, and causes them to be concerned only with Him and for Him." Abū Yazīd said: "If a single atom of the Prophet manifested itself to creation, naught that is beneath the Throne would endure it." He also said: "The gnosis and knowledge of men is, compared with the Prophet's, like the drop of moisture

[1] S. iii. 106.

which oozes out of the top of a bound waterskin." One of them said: "None of the prophets attained the perfection of assent (*taslīm*) and submission (*tafwīḍ*), except the Beloved[1] and the Friend[2]." For this reason, the great Ṣūfīs despaired of attaining perfection, even though they were in the state of nearness (to God), and had experienced true contemplation. Abu 'l-'Abbās ibn 'Aṭā said: "The least of the stages of the messengers is the highest of the ranks of the prophets, and the least of the stages of the prophets is the highest of the ranks of the true believers, and the least of the stages of the true believers is the highest of the ranks of the martyrs, and the least of the stages of the martyrs is the highest of the ranks of the pious, and the least of the stages of the pious is the highest of the ranks of the believers."

Chapter XXV

THEIR DOCTRINE OF THE FAULTS ASCRIBED TO THE PROPHETS

Al-Junayd, Al-Nūrī and others of the great Ṣūfīs hold that whatever happened to the prophets only affected them outwardly, and that their secret hearts were absorbed with the contemplations of God. They cite in support of this view the words of God: "But he forgot it, and we found no purpose in him."[3] They say that acts are not genuine, unless they are preceded by resolves and intentions, and that if something is without resolve and intention, then it is not a deed: God denies this in the case of Adam when He says, "But he forgot it, and we found no purpose in him." When God censured them for such things, it was only in order to serve as a mark for other men, so that they might

[1] Adam. [2] Abraham. [3] S. xx. 114.

know, when they are disobedient (to God), that they have the chance of seeking God's forgiveness. Others, however, admit these faults (in the prophets), explaining, however, that they were slips arising out of faulty interpretation:[1] they were censured for this because their rank was so high and their stations so exalted; and this was intended to serve as a warning to others, and an instruction, to preserve the title to superiority which the prophets have over other men. Some Ṣūfīs say that these faults are to be regarded as instances of forgetfulness and heedlessness, explaining that they were forgetful of the lower thing because of (their pre-occupation with) the higher: so they say, in connection with the occasion when the Prophet forgot to pray, that he was pre-occupied with something greater than prayer; for he said, "I have set my delight in prayer." With these words he informs us that there is something in prayer which delights him: he did not say, "I have made prayer my delight". Those, however, who assert that the Prophets were subject to faults and errors only reckon them as minor sins closely allied to repentance: so God says, when speaking of His elect Adam and his wife, "O our Lord! we have wronged ourselves",[2] and again, "And He turned towards him, and guided him";[3] and of David He says, "And he thought that we were trying him; and he asked pardon of his Lord and fell down bowing, and did turn".[4]

[1] *Ta'wīl*, that is, the failure to interpret God's message correctly.

[2] S. vii. 22.

[3] S. xx. 120.

[4] S. xxxvii. 23.

Chapter XXVI

THEIR DOCTRINE OF THE MIRACLES OF SAINTS

They are agreed in affirming the miracles[1] of the saints, even though they may enter the category of marvels,[2] such as walking on water, talking with beasts, travelling from one place to another,[3] or producing an object in another place or at another time:[4] all these examples are duly recorded in the stories and traditions, and they are also spoken of in the scriptures. For example, there is the story of "he who had the knowledge of the Book",[5] who said: "I will bring it to thee before thy glance can turn";[6] and the story of Mary, when Zachariah said to her "O Mary! how hast thou this? She said, 'It is from God'."[7] There is also the story of the two men who were with the Prophet, and then went forth, and their whips shone with light. Such things may happen equally both in the time of the Prophet, and at other periods:[8] for as miracles were vouchsafed in the time of the Prophet in order to testify to the truth (of his claim), so they have happened at other periods for a similar reason. After the death of the Prophet, this happened to 'Umar ibn al-Khaṭṭāb, when he called Sāriyah, saying, "O Sāriyah ibn Ḥiṣn, the mountain, the mountain!" 'Umar was then at Medina in the pulpit, and Sāriyah was facing the enemy,

[1] *Karāmāt.* [2] *Mu'jizāt.*

[3] Sc. miraculous journeys, such as that of the Prophet on the occasion of his *mi'rāj*.

[4] Sc. what we should call "apport mediumship".

[5] The commentators exhaust possibilities in trying to identify the name of this person.

[6] S. xxvii. 40. [7] S. iii. 32.

[8] As against the Mu'tazilites, who held the opposite view.

a month's journey away.[1] This story is well authenticated. Those who deny this view do so because they think it implies a slur on the function of the prophet: for a prophet is only distinguished from any other man by the fact that he produces a marvel which proves his veracity, and which other men are incapable of producing; therefore, if it appeared equally well from another person, there would not remain any difference between the prophet and the non-prophet, nor any proof of the prophet's veracity; moreover, it would imply that God is unable to distinguish a prophet from one who is not a prophet. Abū Bakr al-Warrāq, however, said: "A prophet is not a prophet by virtue of some marvel, but because God sent him and made revelation to him. If God has sent a man, and made revelation to him, then he is a prophet, whether he possesses any marvellous powers or not, and it is a duty to accept the claim of a messenger, even if one does not see any marvel proceeding from him: for the real purpose of marvels is, to provide irrefutable proof for those who deny, and to reinforce the threat of punishment in the case of those who are obstinate."[2] The reason for accepting the claim of a prophet is, that he calls men to follow what God Himself has laid down as a duty, namely, the confession of His Unity, together with the denial that He has partners, and the performance of whatever the intellect does not pronounce to be impossible, but rather obligatory or permissible. The fact is, that there are two types involved here, namely, the prophet and the prophetaster.[3] The prophet is truthful, the prophetaster is false: yet in outward appearance and composition they are alike.

They are agreed that God strengthens the truthful

[1] Some MSS. add "at Nahāwand". The date of this event was 21 A.H.

[2] Some MSS. add "in their unbelief".

[3] The word here used is *mutanabbī*, sc. one who falsely claims to be a prophet.

person by means of a marvel, whereas the false man cannot have the same property as the truthful, for that would imply that God is unable to distinguish the truthful from the false. As for the man, however, who is a true saint, but not a prophet, he does not lay claim to be a prophet, or anything that is false or untrue: he only invites men to accept what is true and truthful. If God displays a miraculous power (*karāmah*) in him, this in no way impugns the prophet's office, or throws doubt on it: for the truthful man agrees with the prophet both in words and mission; and the very appearance of miraculous powers in him only reinforces the prophet and manifests his claim, strengthening his proof and right to be accepted in his mission and claim to be a prophet, and also affirms the principle that God is One.

Some of the Ṣūfīs maintain that it may happen that God will cause His enemies to see in their own persons—that is, in such a way as not to provoke doubt (in others)—certain extraordinary powers, with the intention of bringing them gradually to ruin, and leading them to destruction. These powers then produce a conceit and pride in their souls, and they imagine that they are miracles which they have merited by their actions and deserved through their deeds: they talk of their actions, supposing themselves to be superior to other men; they despise God's servants, and behave arrogantly towards them, for they do not suspect what God is plotting. As for saints, however, when any miraculous dispensation is accorded them by God, they are all the more humble, submissive, fearful and lowly towards God, and the more contemptuous of themselves, so that they readily admit the claim God has of them: and this increases their power and strength to perform strenuous works, and augments their gratitude to God for what He has given them.

Prophets, then, are accorded marvels, saints miracles, and the enemies (of God) deceptions. A certain Ṣūfī said: "The miracles accorded to the saints come to them they know not whence: whereas the prophets know (the origin) of their marvels, and speak in confirmation of them. This difference is due to the fact that with saints there is a danger that they may be tempted (by their miracles), as they are not divinely preserved, whereas with prophets, in view of the fact that they are under God's protection, this danger does not exist."

(They explain the difference between miracles and marvels as follows.) The miracle of the saint consists in an answer to prayer, or the completion of a spiritual state, or the granting of power to perform an act, or the supplying of the means of subsistence requisite and due to them, in a manner extraordinary: whereas the marvels accorded to prophets consist either of producing something from nothing, or of changing the essential nature of an object.[1]

Certain of the theologians and Ṣūfīs admit that these marvels may be vouchsafed in the case of false persons, in a manner unknown[2] to them at the time when they make claim to them, but not in such a way as to engender doubt. Examples of this are: the story of how the Nile flowed when the Pharaoh bade it flow;[3] and the story of the Antichrist, as Muḥammad tells it, who will kill a man, and then, as he imagines, will revive him. They explain these two cases by saying that each is claiming what will by no means engender doubt, because their real natures bear ample evidence to the falsity of their claim to divine powers (*rubūbīyah*).

They are at variance as to whether it is possible for a saint to know that he is a saint. One Ṣūfī said: "This is not possible, because such knowledge would put an end to his fear of the issue,[4] thereby implying security

[1] As the producing of water from the hand, or changing a rod into a snake (comm.).

[2] Some MSS. read "known".

[3] The comm. adds, "and stopped when he bade it stop".

[4] Sc. of one's deeds.

(*amn*). Now the implication of security means the end of servanthood: for the servant (of God) is between fear and hope. God says: 'And they called upon us with longing and dread'."[1] The greatest and most important of the Ṣūfīs, however, maintain that it is possible for a saint to be aware of his sainthood: for sainthood is a grace (*karāmah*) from God to man; and it is permissible for a man to be aware of divine graces and favours, for he will then be moved to greater gratitude.

There are two kinds of sainthood. The first is merely a departure from enmity,[2] and in this sense is general to all believers: it is not necessary that the individual should be aware of it, or realise it, for it is only to be regarded in a general sense, as in the phrase, "The believer is the friend (*walī*) of God." The second is a sainthood of peculiar election and choice, and this it is necessary for a man to be aware of and to realise. When a man possesses this, he is preserved from regarding himself, and therefore he does not fall into conceit; he is withdrawn from other men, that is, in the sense of taking pleasure in regarding them, and therefore they do not tempt him. He is saved from the faults inherent in human nature, although the stamp of humanity remains and persists in him: therefore he does not take delight in any of the pleasures of the soul, in such a way as to be tempted in his religion, although natural delights[3] do persist in him. These are the special qualities of God's friendship (*wilāyah*) towards man: and if a man has these qualities, the Enemy[4] will have no means of reaching him, to lead him astray: for God says, "Verily, as for My servants, thou hast no authority over them."[5] Nevertheless, he will not be divinely

[1] S. xxi. 90.

[2] Giving *wilāyah* the literal interpretation of "friendship", that is, to God, as opposed to enmity through disobedience and unbelief.

[3] Such as breathing, eating and sleeping.

[4] Sc. Satan.

[5] S. xv. 42.

preserved from committing lesser or greater sins: but if he falls into either, sincere repentance will be close at hand to him. The prophet, however, is divinely preserved: all are agreed that no major sin can befall him, while some even hold the same as regards minor sins. Moreover, with him the fear of the issue may certainly pass away, without hindrance. The Prophet informed his Companions that they were of the people of Paradise, and in the case of ten of them testified that they were for Paradise: the narrator of this tradition is Sa'īd ibn Zayd, and he was one of the ten named.[1] Now the testimony of the Prophet must be received with acquiescence, tranquillity and belief: and this implies security from change, and an end of the fear of alteration, as a matter of course. Yet there are the well-known stories which are told to illustrate the fear that possessed those (to whose place in Paradise) the Prophet bore witness. Abū Bakr said: "Would that I were a date pecked by the birds." 'Umar said: "Would that I were this straw. Would that I were nothing." Abū 'Ubaydah said: "I wish that I were a ram, and that my people would sacrifice me, and eat my flesh, and sip my broth." 'Ā'ishah said: "Would that I were a leaf of this tree": and yet it was of her that 'Ammār ibn Yāsir bore witness in the pulpit at Al-Kūfah, saying, "I testify that she is the wife of the Prophet in this world and the next." These feelings came to them because they feared that they might be guilty of acts of opposition (to God), out of reverence for God and respect for His power, and because they were ashamed and afraid of Him: for they had too great a reverence for God to oppose Him, even though He should not punish them. So 'Umar said: "What a good man Ṣuhayb is! He would not disobey God,

[1] These were: Abū Bakr, 'Umar, 'Uthmān, 'Alī, Ṭalḥah, Al-Zubayr, Sa'īd ibn Abī Waqqāṣ, Sa'īd ibn Zayd, 'Abdurraḥmān ibn 'Awf and Abū 'Ubaydah ibn al-Jarrāḥ. To 'Ā'ishah 'Ammār bore witness, as related on this page.

even if he did not fear Him." He meant that Ṣuhayb did not withhold from disobeying God because he feared the consequences, but because he respected God, and reverenced His power, and was ashamed before Him. So the fear of those whose sayings we have quoted[1] was not a fear of change or alteration, for to fear that in spite of the Prophet's testimony would imply a doubt in the Prophet's narrations, and that is unbelief; nor was it a fear of punishment in hell, without remaining there eternally, for they knew that they would not be punished for what they did with hell. For whether they committed minor sins, these would be remitted by their refraining from major sins, or in consequence of the affliction that befell them in this world. 'Abdullāh ibn 'Umar relates that Abū Bakr al-Ṣiddīq said: "I was with the Messenger of God when the following verse was revealed: 'Whosoever doeth evil shall be therewith requited.'[2] The Prophet said, 'Shall I not cause thee to recite a verse which has been revealed to me?' I replied, 'Surely, O Messenger of God!' So he made me recite it: and I do not know what befell me, but I felt as though my back had broken, and I stretched myself up. The Prophet thereupon said: 'What ails thee, Abū Bakr?' I replied: 'O Messenger of God! I adjure thee by my father and mother, is there any of us that has not done evil? Verily we shall be requited for what we have done.' The Prophet answered: 'As for thee, Abū Bakr, and the believers, they shall be therewith requited in this world, so that ye will meet God without sins: but as for the rest, God will store up this for them, and they will be therewith requited on the Day of Resurrection'." Or if they committed major sins, then certainly repentance would follow closely upon them, and the Prophet's tidings of Paradise will be fulfilled for them: for this tradition clearly states that Abū Bakr will come

[1] Lit. "concerning whom good tidings were announced".
[2] S. iv. 122.

on the Day of Resurrection without any sin at all. On another occasion the Prophet said to 'Umar: "How knowest thou that God has not considered the men who fought at Badr, and said, 'Do what ye will, for I have forgiven you'?"

Certain authorities maintain that while they were promised Paradise, they were not promised that they should not be punished. If this were true, then they were afraid of hell, even though they knew that they would not remain in it for ever: and in that case, these specially favoured ones[1] are in no way different from other believers, who will certainly be brought out of hell. Now, if it is possible that Abū Bakr and 'Umar will enter hell, in spite of the Prophet describing them as "the lords of the elders of the people of Paradise, both former and latter", then it is possible that Al-Ḥasan and Al-Ḥusayn will likewise (enter hell), in spite of the Prophet describing them as "the lords of the youth of the people of Paradise." If, then, it is possible that God will bring the lords of the people of Paradise into hell, and punish them thereby, it is not possible that anyone will enter Paradise, without first being punished with hell. Further the Prophet said, "As for the people of the higher ranks, those who are beneath them shall see them as ye see a star that rises over the sky's horizon. Verily, Abū Bakr and 'Umar are among them, and they are blest."[2] Now if these two will enter hell, and will be disgraced therein—for God says, "Verily, whomsoever Thou hast made to enter the fire, Thou hast disgraced him"[3]—then how will it fare with others? Again, Ibn 'Umar relates that the Prophet one day entered the mosque with Abū Bakr and 'Umar, one on his right hand and the other on his left; and he

[1] The ten previously referred to.

[2] The commentators vary between this interpretation of the phrase, and the interpretation that it means "and more than that".

[3] S. iii. 189.

held their hands, and said: "Thus shall we be raised up on the Day of Resurrection." If it is possible, then, that these two will enter hell, it is also possible in the case of a third. But the Prophet said: "There shall enter Paradise of my community seventy thousand without reckoning." 'Ukkāshah ibn Miḥṣan al-Asadī said: "O Messenger of God! pray to God that he may make me one of them." The Prophet answered: "Thou art one of them." Now Abū Bakr and 'Umar were more excellent than 'Ukkāshah, for the Prophet described them as "the lords of the elders of the people of Paradise, both former and latter." How is it possible, then, that 'Ukkāshah will enter Paradise without a reckoning, seeing that he is less than they in excellence, if they are in hell? This, surely, is a great error. These traditions, then, make it quite clear that it is not possible that these two men will be punished with hell, in view, especially, of the Prophet's testimony that they are in Paradise. They at any rate are secure: and whatever else may have been said regarding the other eight previously referred to, as to whether it is possible that they are secure, applies only to them, and not to these two.

As for the manner in which other saints became aware (of their places in Paradise), apart from these ten—for they learned of it through the direct communication of the Prophet, whereas the others did not enjoy this privilege, seeing that they did not live at the time of the Prophet—they became aware of it through the special favours which God accorded them as saints: for their inner hearts experienced those spiritual states which are the signs of God's friendship, of His choosing them and drawing them away from other things to Himself, so that their secret hearts become exempt from all incidents, and events and changes, things that would lure them away from Him, no longer happen to them; moreover, they enjoy those visions and revelations which God only reserves for those whom He specially chose for Himself in eternity, and the like of which

He does not grant to His enemies. There is a tradition of the Prophet concerning Abū Bakr al-Ṣiddīq: "He was not your superior by reason of much fasting and prayer, but because of something which was fixed in his breast, or in his heart."[1] This is the meaning of that tradition. This reassures them that they are experiencing in their hearts divine graces and gifts, and that these are real, and not mere deceptions, as was the case with him to whom God brought His signs, and who "stepped away therefrom".[2] They know that the signs of reality cannot be like the signs of deception and deceit, because the signs of deception only affect them outwardly, and consist of something extraordinary happening, which attracts the person thereby deceived, and beguiles him into thinking that they are symptoms of sainthood and nearness (to God), whereas in reality they are deception and expulsion. If it had been possible that God would make the special grace which he bestows on His saints the same as the deceptions by which He leads His enemies down to destruction, this would mean that He might deal with His saints as He deals with His enemies: He might even curse His prophets, and put them far from Him, as He did with the man to whom He brought His signs; and this cannot be said of God. Moreover, if it were possible for the enemies (of God) to enjoy the signs and marks of sainthood and divine election, and if the pointers of sainthood did not in fact point to it, there would be no guide to truth at all. But the signs of sainthood do not merely consist of external decoration and the manifestation of the extraordinary: its true signs are inwardly, and are the experiences which God puts into the secret heart, experiences which are only known to God and to those who enjoy them.

[1] The words "or in his heart" represent a variant in the tradition.
[2] S. vii. 174.

Chapter XXVII

THEIR DOCTRINE OF FAITH

According to the majority of the Ṣūfīs, faith consists of speech, act and intention. The Prophet, according to a tradition of Ja'far ibn Muḥammad on the authority of his ancestors, said: "Faith is a confession with the tongue, a verification with the heart, and an act with the members." They say that the root of faith is a confession with the tongue together with the verification of the heart, and its branch is the practising of the (divine) commandments. They also say that faith resides in the outward and the inward: the inward is one thing, namely, the heart, while the outward is many things.[1]

They are agreed that faith is necessary as much outwardly as inwardly, without being the portion of one part only[2] of the outward: for since the inward's portion of faith is the portion of the whole, so the outward's portion of faith must be the portion of the whole, that is, practising the divine commandments; for this is general to all the outward, even as verification is general to all the inward. They say that faith may be greater or less. Al-Junayd, Sahl and others of the earlier Ṣūfīs taught that verification also may be greater or less. Its being less is really a departure from faith, because it is the verification of what God has related and promised, and the least doubt concerning this is unbelief: its being greater may be reckoned in terms of strength and certainty. The confession of the tongue does not vary, but the practice of the members may be greater or less. One Ṣūfī said: "The term 'believer' is a name of God, for God says, 'the Peace-giver, the Faithful, the Protector'."[3] Through faith God makes the believer

[1] As tongue, mouth, hand, foot, etc.
[2] Sc. the tongue. [3] S. lix. 23.

secure[1] from His punishment. When the believer confesses and verifies, and also performs the works of obligation, refraining from the things forbidden, then he is secure from God's punishment. If a man does nothing of this, then he is eternally in the fire. When a man confesses and verifies, but fails somewhat in practice, it is possible that he will be punished without being punished eternally: he is therefore secure from eternal punishment, but not from any punishment. His security is then incomplete, not perfect: but the security of the man who performs all is complete, and not wanting. It therefore follows that imperfect security follows imperfect faith, since the completion of security is dependent on the completion of faith. The Prophet has described as "weakness" the faith of one who fails to do his whole duty, saying: "Such a man is weaker in faith."[2] This is the man who sees something objectionable, and objects to it inwardly, but not outwardly: so the Prophet states that inward faith without outward faith is a weak faith. He also uses the term "perfection" in this connection, when he says: "That believer is most perfect in faith who is most beautiful in character." Character comprises both outward and inward: he therefore describes as perfect that which is common to both, and as weak that which is not common to both. A certain Ṣūfī said: "Greater and lesser faith is a matter of quality, not of essence: its increase is in respect of goodness, beauty and strength, while its diminution is likewise in respect of these, not in respect of its essence." The Prophet said: "Many men are perfect, but not of women save four."[3] Now this deficiency on the part of other women is not a

[1] It is impossible to reproduce in English the verbal play of the Arabic.

[2] The Tradition runs: "If a man sees aught objectionable, let him change it with his hand, or if he cannot, then with his tongue, or if he cannot, then with his heart."

[3] Sc. Mary, Fāṭimah, K͟hadījah and 'Ā'is͟hah.

matter of their essential natures, but of attribute. He also described them as being deficient in intellect and religion, and explained the latter deficiency as arising from the fact that they omit to pray and fast during their periods. Now "religion" is in fact Islam, and Islam is identical with faith in the view of those who do not regard works as a part of faith.[1] One of the great Ṣūfīs, on being asked what faith is, said: "Faith on the part of God is neither greater nor less; on the part of the prophets it may be greater but not less; on the part of other men it may be greater and less." By the words "on the part of God (it) is neither greater nor less" is meant, that faith is an attribute of God whereby He is qualified. God says: "The Peace-giver, the Faithful, the Protector."[2] Now the attributes of God cannot be described as being greater or less. It is, however, possible that "faith on the part of God" means the faith which He allotted to man in His foreknowledge, which was not greater at the moment of its being manifested, and was not less than that which God had known and allotted to him. The prophets are in the position of enjoying an augmentation from God, through strength, certainty, and the contemplation of the conditions of the unseen: for God says, "And thus did we show Abraham the kingdom of heaven and of the earth, that he should be one of those who are sure."[3] Other believers have increase in their inward parts through strength and certainty, but suffer diminution as regards the branches of faith because of their shortcomings in performing the divine commandments, and because they commit trespasses forbidden to them (by God). Prophets, however, are divinely protected against committing trespasses, and are preserved from shortcomings as to the divine commandments: they may not, therefore, be described as deficient in a single matter.

[1] Therefore the deficiency is only one of attribute, not of essence. [2] S. lix. 23. [3] S. vi. 75.

Chapter XXVIII

THEIR DOCTRINE OF THE REALITIES OF FAITH

One of the Shaykhs said: "The elements of faith are four: unification without limitation, recollection without interruption, state without description, and ecstasy without moment." The words "state (*ḥāl*) without description (*na't*)" mean, that what he describes is also his state, so that he is qualified with every exalted state which he describes: "ecstasy without moment (*waqt*)" means, that he contemplates God at every moment.[1] One Ṣūfī said: "If a man's faith is true, he does not regard phenomena (*kawn*) and phenomenal objects: for baseness of purpose arises from paucity of gnosis." Another said: "True faith is the veneration of God, and the fruits thereof is shame before God." It has been said: "As for the believer, his breast is dilated with the light of Islam, and his heart is turned to his Lord; the interior of his heart (*fu'ād*) witnesses his Lord, and his understanding is sound; he takes his refuge with his Lord, being consumed when He is near, and crying out when He is far." Another said: "Faith in God is the contemplation of His divinity." Abu 'l-Qāsim al-Baghdādī said: "Faith is that which joins thee with God and concentrates thee on God. God is one, and so the believer is one."[2] If a man accords with things, desires separate him: and if a man is separated from God by his desire, and follows his lusts and the things that he desires, he loses God. Dost thou not see that God commanded them to repeat their covenants at every thought and glance? For God says, "O ye who believe! believe."[3] The Prophet said: "Unbelief is

[1] That is, the *ḥāl* is permanent, and so the *waqt*, or moment of divine ecstasy, becomes a permanent condition.

[2] Sc. made one with God.

[3] S. iv. 136.

more hidden among my community than the track of an ant over stones on a dark night." The Prophet also said: "May the money-worshipper perish, may the belly-worshipper perish, may the sex-worshipper perish, may the clothes-worshipper perish." I asked one of our Shaykhs concerning faith, and he said: "It means, that thou shouldst be entirely responsive to the call (of God), removing from thy heart all thoughts of departing from God, so that thou art present with all that is God's, and absent from all that is not God's." On another occasion I asked him the same question, and he said: "Faith is a thing the opposite of which may not be displayed, and the undertaking of which may not be shirked. The words 'O ye who believe!' imply, 'O people of My choice and gnosis! O people of My nearness and contemplation!'" Certain of the Ṣūfīs account faith and Islam to be one; whereas others distinguish between them, saying: "Islam is general, but faith is special." A Ṣūfī said: "Islam is outward, faith is inward." Another said: "Faith is realisation and belief, Islam is humility and subjection." Another said: "Islam is the realisation of faith, faith is the verification of Islam." Another said: "Unitarianism is a secret, and it consists in declaring that God cannot be perceived; gnosis is a piety, and means that thou knowest God in His attributes; faith is a compact of the heart to preserve the secret, and to know the piety; Islam is the contemplation of God's subsistence in everything which is required of thee."

Chapter XXIX

THEIR DOCTRINE OF THE LEGAL SCHOOLS

Regarding matters over which the lawyers differ, the Ṣūfīs pursue the more cautious and conservative course, and wherever possible follow the consensus of the two contesting parties concerned. They hold that the differences between the lawyers make for righteousness, and that neither party is really at conflict with the other.[1] In their view, every man who strives to righteousness is right, and every man who holds a given principle in law as sound, by analogy with similar principles established by the Qur'ān and the Sunna, or through the judicious use of interpretation,[2] is right in holding such belief. If, however, a man is not sufficiently grounded in the law,[3] then he will abide by the decision of such previous lawyers as he feels to be more learned, whose judgment is for him decisive.

They believe in expediting their prayers, this being in their view the more excellent course, provided one is certain of the appropriate moment for performance, and likewise in expediting the observance of all religious duties at their proper season. They do not allow any shortening, postponement or omission, except it be with good cause. They agree that when travelling a man may shorten his prayers, but if he is continually on the move, and has no settled abode, then he must perform the prayers in full. They hold that it is permissible to break one's fast when travelling during a fast. They interpret the principle of "capacity" in connection with the obligation of the pilgrimage[4] in the broadest sense, and do not limit its conditions to the possession of provisions and a mount. Ibn 'Aṭā said: "Capacity consists of two things: condition[5] and wealth. If a man does not possess the condition necessary to support him, then his wealth will help him to achieve."

[1] Their differences are on matters of unimportant detail, and so long as each follows the dictates of his principles, each is right. Cf. the Tradition: "The differences of my community are a mercy."

[2] *Istinbāṭ*, the clearing up of difficult points in law.

[3] *Ijtihād*, the lawyer's fullest exercise of his faculties.

[4] Cf. S. iii. 91.

[5] Sc. spiritual condition, trust in God to provide.

Chapter XXX

THEIR DOCTRINE OF EARNING

They are agreed that it is permissible to acquire earnings from trades, commerce or agriculture, or any other means permitted by the religious law, provided one exercises due caution, deliberation and care to avoid things of doubtful legality: these earnings are to be applied to mutual assistance, the repressing of desires, and in readiness to help others and to be charitable to one's neighbour. They hold that it is compulsory for a man to earn, if he has any dependents whom it is his duty to support. According to Al-Junayd, the proper method of earning, beside the foregoing conditions, is to engage in works which bring one nearer to God, and to occupy oneself with them in the same spirit as with works of supererogation commended to one, not with the idea that they are a means of sustenance or advantage. Others, however, hold that it is permissible, but not necessary, to earn, provided that the individual's trust in God is not in any way impaired, or his religion affected: it is, however, more proper and right to occupy oneself with one's obligations to God, and it is a prior duty to turn away from all acquisition, in perfect trust and faith in God. Sahl said: "It is not proper for those who put all their trust in God[1] to acquire, except for the purpose of following the Sunna; and for others it is not proper, except for the purpose of mutual assistance."

These are the true doctrines of the Ṣūfīs, as far as we have verified them from what is stated in the books of those whose names we mentioned at the beginning, or heard them from reliable authorities who were acquainted with their principles and verified their doctrines, or as far as we have understood the riddles and

[1] Sc. to an exceptional degree, such as the prophets and saints.

veiled references contained in their actual discourse. All this, it is true, is not set down after the fashion in which we have related it. The greater part of the proofs and evidence which we have cited is our own composition, expressive of what we have gathered from their books and treatises: but let any man study and examine their discourse and books, and he will know that what we have related is true. Indeed, but for our being loath to make a long discussion, we would have quoted chapter and verse from their books for every point we have mentioned, for all this is not set down sufficiently clearly in the books.

And now we will mention the special doctrines of the Ṣūfīs, the peculiar expressions which they have used, the sciences which they have studied, and the general purport of their discourse, explaining wherever possible their meanings. Of God we ask assistance, for there is no power nor strength save with God.

Chapter XXXI

OF THE ṢŪFĪ SCIENCES OF THE STATES

I say (and God is my help): Know that the sciences of the Ṣūfīs are the sciences of the spiritual states, and that these states are the heritage of acts, and are only experienced by those whose acts have been right. Now the first step to right conduct is to know the sciences thereof, namely, the legal prescriptions, consisting of the principles of law (*fiqh*) governing prayer, fasting and other religious duties, as well as the social sciences[1] regulating marriage, divorce, commercial transactions, and other matters affecting human life which God has laid down and prescribed as indispensable. These are the sciences which are acquired by learning: and it is a

[1] Lit. "science of methods of conduct".

man's first duty to strive to seek after this science and its rules, as far as he is able to the limit of the capacity of his nature and intellect, after being thoroughly grounded in theology[1] and the use of the Qur'ān, the Sunna, and the consensus of the fathers,[2] to the extent of appreciating the sound doctrine of the congregation of orthodox Muslims.[3] If God helps him to higher achievement than this, that he may drive away all doubts of glance or thought that come upon him, it is well: but even if he turns from evil thoughts by seeking protection of the sum of knowledge which he possesses, and shuns the glance[4] which vies and contends with him and keeps him far (from God), that is ample provision for him, if God wills; for he is occupied in the employment of his knowledge, and practises according to what he knows.[5]

It is first of all necessary, then, that he should know the vices of the soul, and be thoroughly acquainted with the soul, its education, and the training of its character; he must also know the wiles of the Enemy, and the temptations of this world, and how to eschew them.[6] This science is the science of wisdom (*ḥikmah*). When the soul is properly addressed, and its habits amended, when it is schooled in the divine manners, reining its members, and guarding its fingers and all its senses, then it is easy for a man to amend its character and purify its outward part,[7] so that it is no more occupied with its own affairs, and shuns and

[1] *Tawḥīd.* [2] Lit. "the pious men of old".

[3] Lit. "the people of the Sunna and the congregation".

[4] Sc. at other than God.

[5] Cf. the Tradition: "If a man practises according to what he knows, God will bequeath him the knowledge of what he does not know."

[6] This follows closely the teaching of Muḥāsibī in his *Muḥāsabat al-nufūs*.

[7] The "divine manners" are the prescriptions of the Sunna: the "outward part" of the soul means its dealings with the outside world.

turns away from this world. Thereafter that man is able to watch over the thoughts, and purify the inward parts: and this is the science of gnosis. Beyond this are the sciences of thoughts, the sciences of contemplations and revelations: these sciences are entirely comprised in the science of allusion (*ishārah*), and this is the science *par excellence* of the Ṣūfīs, which they acquire after they have mastered all the sciences which we have mentioned. The term "allusion" is given to this science for this reason: the contemplations enjoyed by the heart, and the revelations accorded to the conscience (*sirr*), cannot be expressed literally; they are learnt through actual experience of the mystical, and are only known to those who have experienced these mystical states and lived in these stations. Sa'īd ibn al-Musayyib relates on the authority of Abū Hurayrah that the Prophet said: "Verily, a part of knowledge is after the fashion of something hidden: it is only known by those who are acquainted with God. When they speak about it, it is only disapproved of by those who are heedless of God." The following narrative goes back to 'Abdu 'l-Wāḥid ibn Zayd: "I asked al-Ḥasan about the science of the inward, and he said, 'I asked Ḥudhayfah ibn al-Yamān about the science of the inward, and he said, I asked the Messenger of God about the science of the inward, and he said, I asked Gabriel about the science of the inward, and he said, I asked God about the science of the inward, and He said, It is a secret of My secret: I set it in the heart of My servant, and none of My creatures understands it'." Abu 'l-Ḥasan ibn Abī Dharr quotes the following verses of Al-Shiblī in his book, the *Minhāj al-dīn*:

The science of the Ṣūfīs has no bound,
A science high, celestial, divine:
In it the Masters' hearts have plunged profound,
And men of wit appraise them by that sign.

Now every station has a beginning and an end: and between these two are the various states. Every station has its own science, and every state its own allusion. In every station there is an affirmation and a denial: but not all that is denied in one station is denied in the station before it, nor is all that is affirmed in one station affirmed in the station after it. This is in keeping with the saying of the Prophet, "If a man has no faithfulness, then he has no faith." Here he is referring to the faith of faithfulness, not the faith of religious belief. Now those who were thus addressed perceived this, for they had either dwelt in the station of faithfulness, or had passed beyond and above it: the Prophet understood their spiritual states, and so made himself clear to them. Now if a man discoursing does not take account of the spiritual conditions of his hearers, but expounding a certain station denies and affirms, it is possible that there may be in his audience one who has never dwelt in that station: what he denies may be affirmed in the station of that hearer, so that he will imagine that the speaker has denied something which knowledge affirms, and that he has either made a mistake, or fallen into heresy, or even perhaps relapsed into unbelief. This being so, the Ṣūfīs invented technical expressions for their sciences which they understood among themselves: these they used as a code, which was grasped by their fellow-Ṣūfīs, but escaped any listener who had never dwelt in the same station. The latter then did one of two things: either he thought well of the speaker, and accepted him, convicting himself of lacking sufficient understanding to grasp his meaning; or else he thought ill of the speaker, and accounted him mad, ascribing what he said to lunatic ravings; and even if he did the latter, this was better for him than rejecting and denying a truth.[1] A certain scholastic theologian said to Abu 'l-'Abbās ibn 'Aṭā: "What is it with you Ṣūfīs? Ye have invented terms with which ye entreat your listeners strangely, and ye

[1] As would have been the case if clear argumentation had been used, leaving him no excuse for refusing to acquiesce.

depart from the accustomed speech. Is this for any other purpose but to seek to confuse, or to conceal a vicious doctrine?" Abu 'l-'Abbās replied: "We only did this because we were jealous of Him, and because of His power over us, so that others should not taste (the joys expressed by) these (terms)." Then he began to recite these verses:

This is the fairest thing that ever God revealed,
And we reveal, yet to ourselves keep most concealed:
A dawning truth which, lover-like, speaks lip to lip.
In its own radiance I wrap it closely round,
And hide it, lest one, knowing naught of things profound,
Uncover it, and with uncouth expressions strip
Its spiritual beauty: or, not having wit
To understand, nay, not so much as a tenth part,
He will go taking all in hand, and publish it;
And ignorance will spread abroad its lying bands,
And knowledge will be lost forever, and its art
Will disappear, its path buried in shifting sands.

The following verses are also attributed to the same:

When men of common parlance question us,
We answer them with signs mysterious
And dark enigmas: for the tongue of man
Cannot express so high a truth, whose span
Surpasses human measure; but my heart
Has known it, and has known of it a rapture
That thrilled and filled my body, every part.
Seëst thou not, these mystic feelings capture
The very art of speech, as men who know
Vanquish and silence their unlettered foe.

Chapter XXXII

OF THE NATURE AND MEANING OF ṢŪFISM

I heard Abu 'l-Ḥasan Muḥammad ibn Aḥmad al-Fārisī say: "The elements of Ṣūfism are ten in number. The first is the isolation of unification; the second is the understanding of audition; the third is good fellowship; the fourth is preference of preferring; the fifth is the yielding up of personal choice; the sixth is swiftness of ecstasy; the seventh is the revelation of the thoughts; the eighth is abundant journeying; the ninth is the yielding up of earning; the tenth is the refusal to hoard."

Isolation of unification means that no thought of polytheism or atheism should corrupt the purity of the belief in one God. The understanding of audition implies that one should listen in the light of mystical experience, not merely in the light of learning.[1] The preference of preferring means that one should prefer that another should prefer,[2] so that he may have the merit of preferring. Swiftness of ecstasy is realised when the conscience is void of anything that may disturb ecstasy, and not filled with thoughts which prevent one from listening to the promptings of God. The revelation of the thoughts means that one should examine every thought that comes into his conscience, and follow what is of God, but leave alone what is not of God. Abundant journeying is for the purpose of beholding the warnings that are to be found in heaven and earth: for God says, "Have they not journeyed on in the land and seen how was the end of those before them?"[3] and again, "Say, Journey ye on in the land, and behold how the creation appeared";[4] and the words "journey ye on in the land" are explained as meaning, with the light of gnosis, not with the darkness of agnosia, in order to cut the bonds (of materialism) and to train the soul. The yielding up of earning is with a view to demanding of the soul that it should put its trust in God. The refusal to hoard is only meant to apply to the condition of mystical experience, and not

[1] Sc. as to the recitation of mystical poetry, where the true sense is often at variance with the literal meaning.

[2] That is, that one should be eager to teach others the more excellent way of self-abnegation.

[3] S. xxx. 8.

[4] S. xxix. 19.

to the prescriptions of theology. So, when one of the people of the Bench died, leaving behind him a dīnār, the Prophet said concerning him: "A brand for the burning!"[1]

Chapter XXXIII

OF THE REVELATION OF THE THOUGHTS

One of the Shaykhs said: "There are four kinds of thoughts: from God, from an angel, from self, and from the Devil. The thought which is from God is an admonition; that from an angel an urge to obedience; that from self the quest of lust; that from the Devil the bedizenment of disobedience. By the light of unification the thought from God is received, and by the light of gnosis the thought from the angel is received: by the light of faith (the thought of) the self is denied, and by the light of Islam (the thought of) the Devil is rejected."

Chapter XXXIV

OF ṢŪFISM AND BEING AT EASE WITH GOD

Al-Junayd said: "Ṣūfism is the preservation of the moments: that is, that a man does not consider what is outside his limits,[2] does not agree with any but God, and only associates with his proper moment[3]." Ibn

[1] The giving up of all possessions is not a prescription of religion, for even the most pious have left for their children adequate provision: it is intended as a measure of self-discipline, and understood as such.

[2] Sc. his limitations as a man.

[3] "Moment" here has the mystical sense of the immediate spiritual condition: the mystic only occupies himself with the actual.

'Aṭā said: "Ṣūfism means being at ease with God." Abu Ya'qūb al-Sūsī said: "The Ṣūfī is the man who is never made uneasy when aught is taken from him, and never wearies himself with seeking (what he does not possess)." Al-Junayd was asked, "What is Ṣūfism?" He replied: "It is the cleaving of the conscience to God: and this is not attained, save when the soul passes away from secondary causes (*asbāb*), through the power of the spirit, and remains with God." Al-Shiblī was asked: "Why are the Ṣūfīs called Ṣūfīs?" He answered: "Because they have been stamped with the existence of the image and the affirmation of the attribute. If they had been stamped with the effacement of the image, only He would have remained, Who imposes the image and affirms the attribute, and poured their images upon them,[1] but does not approve that any man who truly knows should have either image or attribute." Abū Yazīd said: "The Ṣūfīs are children in the lap of God." Abū 'Abdillāh al-Nibājī said: "Ṣūfism is like the disease *birsām*:[2] in the first stages the patient raves, but when the disease takes a hold on him, it makes him dumb." He means, that the Ṣūfī at first describes his station and speaks as his state demands; but when revelation is granted to him, he is bewildered, and holds his tongue. I heard Fāris say: "So long as ideas appear in a man's thoughts,[3] according to the dictates of the soul's vagaries, he finds it in his heart to esteem the former state higher, and so it comes that he divulges: but as for attainment, it throws a veil over the means of satisfaction, and so he is in the end dumb to every appetite." When Al-Nūrī was asked about Ṣūfism, he said: "It is a divulging of a station, and an attainment of a stature." Being asked to describe their (sc. Ṣūfīs') characteristics, he said: "They bring joy into (the

[1] Other MSS. read *a'alla-hum*, sc. "accounted the image a fault in them". If this is right, then the following words are perhaps the comment of the author.

[2] A tumour of the stomach.

[3] Read *khawāṭiri-hi*.

hearts of) others, and turn away from (the desire of) harming them. God says, 'Take to pardon, and order what is kind, and shun the ignorant'."[1] By "a divulging of a station" he means, that the Ṣūfī, if he expresses himself at all, does so in connection with his own spiritual state, and not with regard to that of any other person, theoretically:[2] and by "an attainment of a stature"[3] he signifies that such a man is transported by his own state through his own state, away from the state of any other person. The following verses of Al-Nūrī are also apposite:

"Speak not of this", Thou saidst,
Then into speechless mysteries Thou ledst
My wondering soul:
Can utterance describe th'unutterable?

Not every man that cries,
"Lo, thus am I!" Thou tak'st at his surmise;
When deeds have shown
That so he is, then claimest Thou thine own.

Now it is our intention to describe some of the stations in the language of the Ṣūfīs themselves, but not at great length, for we have no love of long speech. We will relate of the discourses of the Shaykhs only such as are easy to understand, avoiding dark enigmas and fine-drawn allusions. We will commence with repentance.

Chapter XXXV

THEIR DOCTRINE OF REPENTANCE

Al-Junayd was asked, "What is repentance?" He replied: "It is the forgetting of one's sin." Sahl, being asked the same question, said: "It consists of not for-

[1] S. vii. 198.
[2] Sc. he talks only of personal experience, and does not presume to criticise others according to a preconceived theory.
[3] Or, "a stay".

getting one's sin." This saying of Al-Junayd means, that the sweetness of such an act so entirely departs from the heart, that there remains in the conscience not a trace of it, and one is then as though one had never known it. Ruwaym said: "The meaning of repentance is, that thou shouldst repent of repentance." This is similar in meaning to the saying of Rābi'ah: "I ask pardon of God for my little sincerity in saying, I ask pardon of God." Al-Ḥusayn al-Maghāzilī, being asked concerning repentance, said: "Dost thou ask concerning the repentance of conversion, or the repentance of response?" The other said: "What is the repentance of conversion?" Ruwaym answered: "That thou shouldst fear God because of the power He has over thee." The other asked: "And what is the repentance of response?" Ruwaym replied: "That thou shouldst be ashamed before God because He is near thee." Dhu 'l-Nūn said: "The repentance of the common is from sin; the repentance of the elect is from forgetfulness; the repentance of prophets is from seeing that they are unable to reach what others have attained." Al-Nūrī said: "Repentance means, that thou shouldst turn from everything but God." Ibrāhīm al-Daqqāq said: "Repentance means, that thou shouldst be unto God a face without a back, even as thou hast formerly been unto Him a back without a face."[1]

Chapter XXXVI

THEIR DOCTRINE OF ABSTINENCE

Al-Junayd said: "Abstinence is when the hands are void of possessions, and the heart of acquisitiveness." 'Alī ibn Abī Ṭālib, being asked what the nature of abstinence is, replied: "It means, that one does not

[1] That is, he then turns to God all the time, just as before he turned away from God all the time.

care who consumes (the things of) this world, be he believer or unbeliever." Yaḥyā said: "Abstinence is the quitting of what may be dispensed with." Ibn Masrūq said: "Apart from God, no secondary cause possesses the abstinent man." Al-Shiblī, being asked concerning abstinence, said: "Alas for you! What value is there in that which is less than the wing of a gnat, that abstinence must needs be exercised concerning it?"[1] Abū Bakr al-Wāsiṭī said: "Why art thou so impetuous over quitting a vile place,[2] or how long wilt thou be zealous in turning from that which weighs not with God so much as the wing of a gnat?" Al-Shiblī, being asked again concerning abstinence, said: "In reality there is no such thing as abstinence: if one is abstinent regarding what does not belong to him, that is not abstinence; and if one is abstinent regarding what does belong to him, how can that be called abstinence, when it is yet with him and he with it? It consists of restraining the appetite, being generous, and doing good."[3] It is as if he construes abstinence to mean leaving something which does not belong to one: and if something does not belong to one, one cannot properly leave it, because it is already left; while if something does belong to one, then it is not possible to leave it.

Chapter XXXVII

THEIR DOCTRINE OF PATIENCE

Sahl said: "Patience is the expectation of consolation from God: it is the noblest and highest of services." Another said: "Patience means being patient with

[1] Referring to the well-known Tradition, "This world does not weigh with God so much as a gnat's wing": *vid.* Wensinck, *Concordance*, p. 200.

[2] Literally, "latrine".

[3] These two words imply, first giving away what one possesses, then restoring what rightfully belongs to another.

patience." This signifies, that one should not look for any consolation therein. Another composed these verses:

With patience patiently he bore,
Till patience for his succour cried:
And, being schooled in patience' lore,
"O patience, patience!" he replied.

Sahl said: "The words of God, 'Seek aid of patience and prayer',[1] mean, Seek aid of God, and be patient with God's command and God's practices." Sahl also said: "Patience is blessed, and with it things are blessed." Abū 'Amr al-Dimashqī commented on the words of God, "Harm has touched me"[2] thus: "Harm has touched me, and taught me patience, because Thou art 'the most merciful of the merciful'." Another said: "He (sc. Job) was only impatient for God's sake, not on his own account: this was because the distress had taken such a hold of his body, that he feared his reason might fail." They quote the following verses of Abu 'l-Qāsim Sumnūn in this connection:

Well have I quaffed time's water-skin,
And tasted all its joy and pain;
Yea, I have pressed its mouthpiece in
My lips, and sucked out every drain.

And destiny has poured its cup
Of griefs, which drinking, from my sea
Of patience I have filled it up
And passed it back to destiny.

With patience I am shod, and roll
Time's chances round me for a dress,
Crying, "Have patience, O my soul!
Or thou wilt perish of distress."

So huge a mass my sufferings are
That mountains, trembling at its height,
Would vanish, like a headlong star
And evermore be lost to sight.[3]

[1] S. ii. 42.
[2] S. xxi. 83. Job is speaking.
[3] I have translated these verses rather freely in some particulars, in an attempt to provide more English metaphors. Their meaning, however, is quite clear.

Chapter XXXVIII

THEIR DOCTRINE OF POVERTY

Abū Muḥammad al-Jurayrī said: "Poverty means that one should not seek the non-existent until one has failed to find the existent." He means, that one should not seek the means of sustenance, unless one fears that he will not be able to perform a religious duty. Ibn al-Jallā said: "This is poverty, that there should be nothing that is thine; and even if there is something, that it should not be thine."[1] This saying bears the same meaning as the words of God, "And they prefer them to themselves, even though there be poverty among them."[2] Abu Muḥammad Ruwaym ibn Muḥammad said: "Poverty is the non-existence of every existent thing, and the abandonment of every lost thing." Al-Kattānī said: "When a man is truly in need of God, then he is truly rich in God: neither of these states is complete without the other." Al-Nūrī said: "The description of the poor man is, that he should be quiet when he possesses nothing, and generous and unselfish when he possesses something." One of the great Ṣūfīs said: "The poor man is forbidden ease, and also forbidden to ask. So the Prophet said, 'If he had adjured by God, God would have fulfilled it',[3] indicating that he would not so adjure." Al-Darrāj said: "I examined the sleeve of my master, looking for a kohl-box, and I found in it a piece of silver. I was astonished thereat, and when he came I said to him: 'Lo, I found a piece (of silver) in thy sleeve!' He replied: 'I have seen it. Give it back.' Then he said: 'Take it, and buy something with it.' I asked: 'What was the purpose of this piece, in view of the rights of Him thou wor-

[1] Sc. that thou shouldst rather reckon it as belonging to others, and so give it away.

[2] S. lix. 9.

[3] A famous Tradition: *vid.* Wensinck, *Concordance*, p. 159.

shippest?' He answered: 'God provided me with nothing yellow or white[1] in this world, save this; and I intended to make deposition that it should be wrapped in my winding-sheet, so that I could give it back to God'."

I heard Abu 'l-Qāsim al-Baghdādī tell the following anecdote which he heard from Al-Dawrī: "On the night of the festival[2] we were in the company of Abu 'l-Ḥusayn al-Nūrī, in the Shūnīzī mosque. A man came up to us and said to Al-Nūrī, 'Master, tomorrow is the festival. What wilt thou wear?' Al-Nūrī began to recite these verses:

'Tomorrow is the festival!' they cried,
'What robe wilt thou put on?' And I replied:
'The robe He gave me, Who hath poured for me
Full many a bitter potion. Poverty
And patience are my garments, and they cover
A heart that sees at every feast its Lover.
Can there be finer garb to greet the Friend,
Or visit Him, than that which He doth lend?
When Thou, my Expectation, art not near,
Each moment is an age of grief and fear:
But while I may behold and hear thee, all
My days are glad, and life's a festival!'"

One of the great Ṣūfīs[3] was asked: "What has prevented the rich from bestowing of the superfluity of their possessions upon this sect?" He replied: "Three things. The first is, that that which they possess is not good: now the Ṣūfīs are God's elect; and that which has been chosen for the people of God is accepted (by God), but God only accepts what is good. The second is, that the Ṣūfīs are deserving (of the divine reward), and so others are not permitted the blessing of having helped them, and the reward on their account. The third is, that they are intended for suffering, and there-

[1] Sc. gold or silver.
[2] That is, the night ending Ramaḍān and beginning Bairām.
[3] The commentator assigns this anecdote to Abū Sa'īd al-Kharrāz, quoting Qushayrī, *Risālah*, p. 160 (ed. Cairo, 1284).

fore God prevents their being helped in order that His intention concerning them may be realised." Fāris told me the following: "I saw a certain poor man,[1] who bore the marks of hunger, and I said to him: 'Why dost thou not ask of men, that they may give thee to eat?' He replied: 'I fear to ask them, lest they refuse me, and not prosper. I have heard that the Prophet said, If the beggar were sincere, he who refused him would not prosper'."

Chapter XXXIX

THEIR DOCTRINE OF HUMILITY

Al-Junayd was asked concerning humility, and he said: "It consists of lowering the wing[2] and contracting the side." Ruwaym said: "Humility is the abasement of the heart to Him Who knoweth the unseen." Sahl said: "The perfection of the recollection of God is contemplation, and the perfection of humility is being well pleased with God." Another said: "Humility is accepting the truth from the Truth for the Truth."[3] Another said: "Humility is taking pride in constriction, adhering to submission, and shouldering the burdens of the people of religion."

Chapter XL

THEIR DOCTRINE OF FEAR

Abū 'Amr al-Dimashqī said: "The man of fear fears himself more than he fears the Enemy."[4] Aḥmad ibn al-Sayyid Ḥamdawayh said: "The fearful man is feared

[1] Sc. a Ṣūfī.

[2] Cf. S. xv. 88, etc. This is the Qur'ānic metaphor for humility.

[3] Reminiscent of Junayd.

[4] This saying is attributed by Sarrāj (*Kitāb al-Luma'*, p. 61) to Ibn Khubayq.

by things that cause (others) to fear."[1] Abū 'Abdillāh ibn al-Jallā said: "The fearful man is he of whom are reassured the things that cause fear."[2] Ibn Khubayq said: "The fearful man is subject to the conditions of each (mystical) moment. At one time he is feared by the things that cause fear, and at another they are reassured of him."[3] The man who is feared by the things that cause fear is one over whom fear prevails to such an extent that he becomes entirely fear, and everything fears him. So it is said: "Whoso fears God, is feared by everything." The man of whom the things that cause fear are reassured is such, that when those things strike against his recollections, they have no influence over him, for the fear of God causes him to be unconscious of them; and when a man is unconscious of things, they are also unconscious of him. The following verses give point to this:

> Him the fire burns, who doth the fire discern;
> But he who is the fire—how shall he burn?

Ruwaym said: "The fearful man is he who fears naught but God." He means, that he fears God, not for his own sake, but in reverence to God. Fear for one's own sake is only fear of the issue. Sahl said: "Fear is male, and hope is female." He means, that of these twain are born the realities of faith. He also said: "If a man fears other than God, and hopes for God, God gives him security for fear, and he is veiled."

[1] Reading with V., though the other reading, "created things", may well be correct.

[2] I.e. they do not fear him. To this authority Sarrāj (*loc. cit.*) assigns the saying given a little later by Kalābādhī to Ruwaym.

[3] This saying is quoted by Sarrāj (*loc. cit.*), and I have now preferred the reading of N.V.B., which also has the support of A.B. of Sarrāj.

Chapter XLI

THEIR DOCTRINE OF PIETY

Sahl said: "Piety consists of contemplating the states on the footing of isolation." He means that one should fear what is other than God, having repose in God, and finding pleasure in Him. God's words, "Then fear God as much as ye can",[1] mean, Fear Him with all your power. Sahl said: "'As much as ye can' exhibits need and want of him." Muḥammad ibn Sinjān[2] said: "Piety means leaving everything except God." Sahl explained the words of God, "But the piety from you will reach to Him",[3] as follows: "This is, exemption and sincerity." Another said: "The foundation of piety is the avoidance of what is forbidden, and disassociation from the soul: the more they have done without the pleasures of their souls, the more they have attained certainty." These verses are attributed to Al-Nūrī:

O God, I fear Thee: not because
  I dread the wrath to come; for how
Can such affright, when never was
  A friend more excellent than Thou?

Thou knowest well the heart's design,
  The secret purpose of the mind;
And I adore thee, Light Divine,
  Lest lesser lights should make me blind.

Chapter XLII

THEIR DOCTRINE OF SINCERITY

Al-Junayd said: "Sincerity is that whereby God is desired, whatever the act may be." Ruwaym said: "Sincerity is lifting one's regard from the deed."

[1] S. lxiv. 16. [2] Some MSS. give Subḥān. [3] S. xxii. 38.

I heard Fāris relate that a number of poor men from Khurāsān came to Abū Bakr al-Qaḥṭabī, who addressed them thus: "How commandeth you your Shaykh?"—meaning Abū 'Uthmān. They answered: "He commands us to be obedient much, but always to keep in sight our shortcomings therein." Abū Bakr replied: "Fie on him! Does he not command you to be unconscious of your obedience, in the vision of Him Who is the Originator of your obedience?" A man said to Abu 'l-'Abbās ibn 'Aṭā: "What act is sincere?" He replied: "That which is free from faults." Abū Ya'qūb al-Sūsī said: "The act which is truly sincere is that which is known neither by any angel, to record it, nor by any devil, to corrupt it, nor by the soul, to take pride in it." He means that a man must detach himself entirely for God's sake, and turn from the act to Him.

Chapter XLIII

THEIR DOCTRINE OF GRATITUDE

Al-Ḥārith al-Muḥāsibī said: "Gratitude is God's increase for the grateful." He means, that when a man is grateful, God augments his blessing, and so he is augmented in gratitude. Abū Sa'īd al-Kharrāz said: "Gratitude means acknowledging the Benefactor, and confessing (His) lordship." Abū 'Alī al-Rudhabārī said:

If all my members had a tongue
To laud Thee for thy bounteous care,
Each anthem would new bounties bear,
And Thy whole praise be never sung.

One of the great Ṣūfīs said: "Gratitude consists in being unconscious of gratitude through the vision of the Benefactor." Yaḥyā ibn Mu'ādh said: "Every benefaction from God necessitates gratitude, and this is without end." The following verses are attributed to Abu 'l-Ḥusayn al-Nūrī:

Lord, I will thank Thee: not that I
Can e'er requite Thy love thereby,
But that it may be said of me,
"He took God's bounties gratefully."

Each glorious hour I spent with Thee
Has now become my memory:
For this is gratitude's last treasure,
The joy of recollected pleasure.

One of the great Ṣūfīs used to say in his prayers: "O God, Thou knowest that I am not able to thank Thee according to all Thy bounties: wherefore, I pray Thee, thank Thyself for me."

Chapter XLIV

THEIR DOCTRINE OF TRUST

Sarī al-Saqaṭī said: "Trust is the stripping off of power and strength."[1] Ibn Masrūq said: "Trust is resignation to the course of the decrees of fate." Sahl said: "Trust is being at ease before God." Abū 'Abdillāh al-Qurashī said: "Trust is abandoning every refuge except God." Al-Junayd said: "The reality of trust is, that a man should be God's in a way he has never been, and that God should be his as He has ever been." Abu Sa'īd al-Kharrāz said: "The Lord granted sufficiency to the people of His kingdom, and they dispensed with the stations of trusting in God in order that He might suffice them: for how unseemly a thing it is for the people of purity to make stipulation." He regards putting one's trust in God for the sake of being sufficiently supplied as a stipulation that God will do the necessary supplying.[2] Al-Shiblī said: "Trust is a seemly mendacity." Sahl said: "All the stations have

[1] By saying, and believing, that "there is no power or strength save with God".

[2] And therefore a debased form of trust.

a face and a back, with the exception of trust: trust is a face without a back." He refers to the trust that is of care (for God), not the trust that is for sufficiency (from God): that is, the trust that seeks no recompense from God. One Ṣūfī said: "Trust is a secret shared only by the servant and God." This saying has the same purport as another, attributed to one of the great Ṣūfīs: "Real trust is the abandonment of trust, and that means, that God should be unto them as He was when they were not yet brought into being." A great Ṣūfī said to Ibrāhīm al-Khawwāṣ: "To what has thy Ṣūfism brought thee?" He answered: "To trust." The other said: "Fie upon thee! Thou still strivest for the comfort of thy belly." He meant that putting one's trust in God for one's own sake was merely a way of guarding against some unpleasantness that might befall.

Chapter XLV

THEIR DOCTRINE OF SATISFACTION

Al-Junayd said: "Satisfaction is the relinquishing of free-will." Al-Ḥārith al-Muḥāsibī said: "Satisfaction is quietness of heart under the course of destiny." Dhu 'l-Nūn said: "Satisfaction is the heart's delight in the passage of fate." Ruwaym said: "Satisfaction is anticipation of the decrees (of God) with joy." Ibn 'Aṭā said: "Satisfaction is the heart's regard for what God chose for His servant at the beginning of time, for what He chose for him is best." Sufyān said in Rābi'ah's hearing: "O God, be pleased with me!" She said to him: "Art thou not ashamed to ask for the pleasure of One with Whom thou art not thyself pleased?" Sahl said: "When satisfaction is united with (divine) pleasure, then is contentment constant: and 'good cheer for them, and an excellent resort'."[1] He refers in these words to God's saying: "God is well-pleased

[1] S. xiii. 28.

with them, and they with God."[1] This saying means, that satisfaction in this world beneath the courses of the (divine) decrees bequeaths (divine) pleasure in the world to come with what the pens[2] have noted. God says: "And it shall be decided between them in truth; and it shall be said, 'Praise belongs to God, the Lord of the worlds'."[3] This is the declaration of the monotheists of both parties, the people of heaven and the people of hell: as for the unbelievers, they are not permitted to speak the 'Praise', for they are veiled. The following verses of Al-Nūrī are apposite:

Ah! satisfaction is a bitter potion
Quaffed by contentment, when life's dark commotion
Is reckoned for a pleasure: but it brings
The revelation of most holy things,
Ev'n to God's Presence. Ever barren beast
Most greedily at pasturage doth feast.[4]

Chapter XLVI

THEIR DOCTRINE OF CERTAINTY

Al-Junayd said: "Certainty is the removal of doubt." Al-Nūrī said: "Certainty is contemplation." Ibn 'Aṭā said: "Certainty is that which is not touched by opposition through all the time." Dhu 'l-Nūn said: "Everything which the eyes see is related to knowledge, and that which the hearts know is related to certainty." Another said: "Certainty is the eye of the heart." 'Abdullāh said: "Certainty is the joining of the interval, and the severing of what is between the interval." These words bear the same meaning as those of

[1] S. v. 119. [2] Sc. of the recording angels. [3] S. xxxix. 75.
[4] The last hemistich in the Arabic contains one of those brilliant flashes of poetic inspiration which are so typical of Arabic poetry, but so impossible to reproduce in English: the instant imaging of a sublime sentiment into a familiar picture from everyday life. As we would say of a useless beast, "It eats its head off": and so the comparison serves as an exhortation to the life of abstinence and contentment.

Ḥāriṯhah: "And it was as though I beheld the Throne of my Lord coming forth":[1] his vision was joined with the unseen, and the veils between him and the unseen were removed. Sahl said: "Certainty is revelation." So another said: "If the veil had been lifted, I should not have had greater certainty."

Chapter XLVII

THEIR DOCTRINE OF RECOLLECTION

Real recollection consists in forgetting all but the One recollected. So God says: "And remember thy Lord when thou hast forgotten",[2] that is, when thou hast forgotten what is not God, then thou hast remembered God. The Prophet said: "The solitary ones have the precedence." They asked: "Who are the solitary ones, O Messenger of God?" He answered: "Men and women who recollect much."[3] The "solitary" is he who has none other with him. One of the great Ṣūfīs said: "Recollection banishes forgetfulness; and when forgetfulness is removed, then thou art a recollector, even if thou art silent."[4] The following verses are ascribed to Al-Junayd:

I recollected Thee:
Not that my memory
The twinkling of an eye
Suffered Thee to slip by.

I recollected Thee:
But naught can easier be
Than the light-uttered word,
Forgotten soon as heard.

I heard Abu 'l-Qāsim al-Baghdādī relate that he asked one of the great Ṣūfīs: "What ails the souls of the gnostics? They loath recollection, and find joy in

[1] In the famous Tradition: cf. *supr.* [2] S. xviii. 23.

[3] For this well-known Tradition and its interpretation, *vid.* Lane, s.v. *frd.*

[4] Sc. true recollection does not depend on the spoken word: this is the purport of the verses which follow.

reflection: and yet reflection does not bring to any settlement, while recollection has compensations which give joy." He replied: "They make light of the fruits of recollection, for these do not transport them away from their sufferings. Their pride is in the honour that lies beyond reflection, and which has made them oblivious of the pain of their endeavours." By saying that "they make light of the fruits of recollection" he implies that these fruits are all pleasures of the soul, and the gnostics of course have turned away from the soul and its pleasures. Their reflections, however, are upon the majesty, awe, favour and goodness of God: they reflect on what they owe to God, and so reverence Him, while they turn away from the consideration of whatever merit they may have before God, respecting Him. For the Prophet says, speaking on the authority of God: "If a man is so occupied with recollecting Me that he forgets to pray to Me, I grant him a nobler gift than that which I accord to those who petition Me." This saying may be interpreted thus: if a man is so occupied with the contemplation of My majesty that he forgets to recollect Me with his tongue....For the tongue's recollection is entirely petitioning: moreover, the very contemplation of the majesty bewilders him, and cuts him off from recollecting God. This is the sense of the Prophet's words, "I cannot reckon the praise that is Thine." The following verses of Al-Nūrī are quoted in this connection:

So passionate my love is, I do yearn
    To keep His memory constantly in mind;
But O, the ecstasy with which I burn
    Sears out my thoughts, and strikes my memory blind!

And, marvel upon marvel, ecstasy
    Itself is swept away: now far, now near
My lover stands, and all the faculty
    Of memory is swept up in hope and fear.[1]

[1] I have expanded to make clear the implication of "now far, now near": farness inspires hope that God may favour, while nearness causes fear of God's majesty.

Al-Junayd said: "If a man says 'God' without first experiencing contemplation, he is a liar." The truth of this statement is attested by the words of God: "They say, 'We bear witness that thou art surely the Apostle of God'...and God bears witness that the hypocrites are liars."[1] God accuses them of lying, even though the statement they make is a true statement, because it is not based upon contemplation. Another said: "The heart is for contemplation, the tongue for making expression of the contemplation: if a man gives expression without having contemplated, he is a false witness." One of the great Ṣūfīs wrote:

Thou art my troubler, Lord, not memory,
For Thou wouldst purge all memory out of me.
Memory's a veil, and doth with thought unite
To blind my heart, and hide Thee from my sight.

This is the interpretation: Recollection is the attribute of the recollector; therefore, if I am absent when I recollect, the absence is in myself, for it is a man's own qualities that veil him from the contemplation of his Lord. Sarī al-Saqaṭī said: "I accompanied a negro in the desert, and observed that whenever he recollected God, his colour changed to white. I remarked: 'This is marvellous. Every time thou recollectest God, thy covering alters and thy description is changed.' He replied: 'My brother, truly, if thou wouldst recollect God as He should be recollected, thy covering too would alter, and thy description be changed.' Then he began to sing:

So we remembered—yet oblivion
Was not our habit: but a radiance shone,
A magical breeze breathed, and God was near.
Then vanished selfhood utterly, and I
Remained His only, Who with tidings clear
Attests His Being, and is known thereby."

[1] S. lxiii. 1.

The following verses of Ibn 'Aṭā may be quoted:

Remembrance is of divers sorts, I hold.
The first by love and longing is controlled;
The next is the associate of the soul,
And with it mingles, as the lifeless whole
Is by the spirit quickened unto breath;
The next strips off the spirit, and deals death
Now hidden, now discovered; the last towers
High over the head's crown, and all the powers
Of sight and thought, yea, every phantasy
Of mind cannot attain it. Openly
The heart's eye then beholds Him, and doth scorn
Remembrance, as a burden hardly borne.

He divides recollection into several classes. The first is the recollection of the heart, meaning that the One recollected is previously forgotten, and then remembered; the second is the recollection of the qualities of the One remembered; the third is the contemplation of the One remembered. By this last, a man passes away from recollection: for the qualities of the One remembered cause you to pass away from your own qualities, and so you pass away from recollection.

Chapter XLVIII

THEIR DOCTRINE OF INTIMACY

Al-Junayd was asked: "What is intimacy?" He replied: "Intimacy is the removal of nervousness, together with the persistence of awe." Nervousness is removed, he means, because hope is more prevalent than fear.[1] Dhu 'l-Nūn, being asked the same question, said: "Intimacy is the lover's boldness with the Beloved." His saying has the same purport as the words of God's Friend (Abraham): "Show me how Thou wilt revive the dead",[2] and the words of God's Conversant

[1] Some MSS. read "grief": it is, however, quite clear that "fear" is more appropriate. [2] S. ii. 262.

(Moses): "Show me, that I may look on Thee."[1] God's answer, "Thou wilt not see Me", is as it were an excuse,[2] meaning, "Thou art not able." Ibrāhīm al-Māristānī was asked concerning intimacy, and he said: "It is the heart's joy in the Beloved." Shiblī was asked the same, and he replied: "It is thy estrangement from thyself." Dhu 'l-Nūn said: "The lowest station of intimacy is, that a man should be cast into the fire, and yet not be made absent thereby from Him with Whom he has been familiar." A certain Ṣūfī said: "Intimacy means that a man should be so familiar with recollection,[3] that he is absent from the vision of (all) others." Ruwaym is quoted in this connection:

Thy beauty is my heart's delight,
And holds my mind unceasingly:
Thy love hath set me in Thy sight,
Estranged from all humanity.

Thy recollection comes to me
With friendly tidings from the Friend:
"Behold, as He hath promised thee
Thou shalt attain, and gain thy end."

Wherever Thou mayst chance to light,
O Thou Who art my soul's intent!
Thou comest clearly to my sight,
And in my heart art immanent.

Chapter XLIX

THEIR DOCTRINE OF NEARNESS

Sarī al-Saqaṭī was asked: "What is nearness?" He replied: "It is obedience." Another said: "Nearness means that thou art at the same time presumptuous towards Him,[4] and submissive before Him: for God

[1] S. vii. 139.
[2] An excuse, that is, for not granting his prayer, as Abraham's was granted.
[3] Sc. of God.
[4] As a lover is presumptuous towards his beloved.

says, 'Adore and draw nigh'."[1] Ruwaym was asked concerning nearness, and he said: "It puts to an end every obstacle." Another, being likewise asked, replied: "It means that thou witnessest what He has done with thee." The meaning of this saying is, that thou seest His acts and bounties towards thee, and therein art unconscious of thy own acts and endeavours: or it may also imply that thou dost not consider thyself as the agent, according to God's words, "Thou didst not shoot when thou didst shoot, but God did shoot", and, "Ye did not slay them, but it was God Who slew them."[2] Al-Nūrī wrote the following:

I had supposed that, having passed away
From self in concentration, I should blaze
A path to Thee: but ah! no creature may
Draw nigh Thee, save on Thy appointed ways.
I cannot longer live, Lord, without Thee;
Thy hand is everywhere: I may not flee.

Some have desired through hope to come to Thee,
And Thou hast wrought in them their high design:
Lo, I have severed every thought from me,
And died to selfhood, that I might be Thine.
How long, my heart's Beloved? I am spent:
I can no more endure this banishment.

This is the interpretation: My state made me suppose that my concentration on Thee and my passing-away from all other than Thee was a means of drawing near to Thee. But concentration and passing-away are attributes: and nearness to Thee is not attained through any attribute of mine, but only through Thee, in so far as it proceeds from Thee. He continues: Some people have sought to come near Thee by virtue of their deeds and acts of obedience, and Thou didst join them to Thee of Thy bounty. I have no deeds whereby to draw near to Thee, and I am perishing of my longing to be near Thee: yet I have no means of myself to come thither. The following verses are also by Al-Nūrī:

[1] S. xcvi. 19. [2] S. viii. 17.

I saw Him passing by,
And did suppose that He was nigh:
But His demands are grievous; my hopes die.

Then, as despairs descend,
An attestation He doth send
Bright with new miracles that never end.[1]

He says: Whenever I despair as far as concerns myself, the bounty which He has displayed restores me from my despair.

Chapter L

THEIR DOCTRINE OF UNION

Union implies being inwardly separated from all but God, seeing inwardly—in the sense of veneration—none but God, and listening to none but God. Al-Nūrī said: "Union is the revelation of the heart and the contemplation of the conscience." Revelation of the heart is illustrated by the words of Ḥārithah: "It was as though I beheld the Throne of my Lord coming forth",[2] while contemplation of the conscience is indicated by the Prophet's saying: "Worship God as if thou seest Him",[3] and the words of Ibn 'Umar: "We were beholding God in that place."[4] Another said: "Union is when the conscience arrives at the station of oblivion", meaning that veneration for God distracts from the veneration of aught else. One of the great Ṣūfīs said: "Union is when the servant witnesses none but his Creator, and when no thought occurs to his conscience, save it be of his Maker." Sahl said: "They were moved by the affliction, and were therefore in commotion. If they had been at rest, they would have attained union."

[1] I omit the philological note.
[2] *Vide* p. 7, *supra*.
[3] For this famous Tradition, cf. Muslim, *Ṣaḥīḥ*, I, p. 158.
[4] For the full narrative, *vide* p. 119.

Chapter LI

THEIR DOCTRINE OF LOVE

Al-Junayd said: "Love is the inclination of the heart", meaning that the heart then inclines towards God and what is of God, without any effort. Another said: "Love is concord", that is, obedience in what God commands, refraining from what He forbids, and satisfaction with what He has decreed and ordained. Muḥammad ibn 'Alī al-Kattānī said: "Love means preferring the beloved." Another said: "Love means preferring what one loves for the person whom one loves." Abū 'Abdillāh al-Nibājī said: "Love is a pleasure if it be for a creature, and an annihilation if it be for the Creator." By "annihilation" he means, that no personal interest remains, that such love has no cause, and that the lover does not persist through any cause. Sahl said: "Whoso loves God, he is life; but whoso loves,[1] he has no life." By the words "he is life" he means that his life is agreeable, because the lover finds delight in whatever comes to him from the beloved, whether it be loathsome or desirable: while by "he has no life" he means that, as he is ever seeking to reach what he loves, and ever fearing that he may be prevented from attaining it, his whole life is lost. One of the great Ṣūfīs said: "Love is a pleasure, and with God there is no pleasure: for the stations of reality are astonishment, surrender and bewilderment. The love of man for God is a reverence indwelling in his heart, and not countenancing the love of any other than God. The love of God for man is, that He afflicts him, and so renders him improper for any but Him. This is the sense of God's words: 'And I have chosen thee for Myself'."[2] By the words "renders him improper for any but Him"

[1] Some MSS. add "other than God".
[2] S. xx. 43.

he means, that there remains no part over in him wherewith he may attend to other things, or pay heed to material conditions. One of the Ṣūfīs said: "Love is of two kinds: the love of confession, which belongs to elect and common alike, and the love of ecstasy in the sense of attainment. With this latter there is no consideration of self or other creatures, or of secondary causes or conditions, for there is a total absorption in the consideration of what is with God and of God." One of the Ṣūfīs[1] composed these verses:

> Two ways I love Thee: selfishly,
> And next, as worthy is of Thee.
> 'Tis selfish love that I do naught
> Save think on Thee with every thought;
> 'Tis purest love when Thou dost raise
> The veil to my adoring gaze.
> Not mind the praise in that or this,
> Thine is the praise in both, I wis.

Ibn 'Abd al-Ṣamad said: "Love is that which renders blind and deaf: it makes blind to all but the Beloved, so that one beholds no objective but Him. The Prophet said: Thy love is a thing which renders blind and deaf." He also recited the following verses:

> Love deafens me to every voice but His:
> Was ever love so strange as this?
> Love blinds me, and on Him alone I gaze:
> Love blinds and, being hidden, slays.

He also recited:

> There is a superfluity of love
> Which no man may endure: it soars above
> All judgment, when the so much dreaded thing
> Descends. Or let it equal anguish bring,
> He will be glad: or let it pass all measure,
> He will rejoice, and reckon it a pleasure.

[1] These famous verses are generally attributed to Rābi'ah, the woman-mystic. A literal version of them occurs in Miss M. Smith's monograph, *Rābi'a*, p. 102. I have here reproduced the excellent version of R. A. Nicholson: see his *Literary History of the Arabs*, p. 234.

Now the Ṣūfīs have certain peculiar expressions and technical terms which they mutually understand, but which are scarcely used by any others. We will set forth such of these as may be convenient, illustrating their meanings with word and phrase. In this we merely aim at explaining the meaning of the several expressions, not the experience which the expression covers: for such experience does not come within the scope even of reference, much less explanation. The real essence of the spiritual states of the Ṣūfīs is such that expressions are not adequate to describe it: nevertheless, these expressions are fully understood by those who have experienced these states.

Chapter LII

THEIR DOCTRINE OF DETACHMENT AND SEPARATION

The meaning of detachment is, that one should be detached outwardly from accidents, and inwardly from compensations: that is, that one should not take anything of the accidents of this world, nor seek any compensation for what one has thus forsworn, whether it be of temporal or eternal; but rather, that one should do this because it is a duty to God, and not for any other reason or motive. Further, it means that one's conscience should be detached from the consideration of the various stations and states in which one lodges from time to time, in the sense that one feels no satisfaction or attachment to them.

The meaning of separation is, that one should separate oneself from all forms, and be separated in the states and one in the acts: that is, that one's actions should be wholly unto God, and that there should be in them no thought of self, no respect of persons, and no regard for compensation. Moreover, one should be separated in the states from those very states, and so not realise any state at all, being entirely absorbed therefrom in the vision of Him Who appoints the states: and in being separated from all forms,[1] one should neither associate with them, nor seek to be estranged from them. It has been said: "Detachment means that one does not possess, separation means that one is not possessed." The following verses of 'Amr ibn 'Uthmān al-Makkī illustrate:

Alone with a lone God he is alone:
One he remains, for his Desire is One.
So I have seen them, each in his degree,
Those solitary seekers; and lo, he
That travels farthest nearest is to goal.[2]
One from the witnessed world, with zeal of soul,
Turns, and soars upwards, upwards in his flight
Alone, alone in all his suffering.
Another upwards from his soul doth spring
In lonely ecstasy. Another breaks
The clinging bonds of selfhood, and awakes
Alone, yet not alone: the bounteous Lord
Receives His own elect with love outpoured.

The man who "soars upwards, upwards in his flight alone" is "alone in all his suffering" because he cannot find any way of reaching his quest, and will not rest in anything short of it. The man who "upwards from his soul doth spring in lonely ecstasy" does not feel this suffering. Finally, he who "breaks the clinging bonds of selfhood" through passing away from self is the man chosen and brought near (by God), and he is alone with the Reality.

[1] Evidently with the sense "other men".
[2] This appears to be the intention of a very obscure conceit.

Chapter LIII

THEIR DOCTRINE OF ECSTASY

Ecstasy is a sensation which encounters the heart, whether it be fear, or grief, or the vision of some fact of the future life, or the revelation of some state between man and God. They say: "And it is the hearing and sight of the heart." God says: "For it is not their eyes which are blind, but blind are the hearts which are within their breasts",[1] and again: "Or gives ear, and is a witness thereto."[2] If a man's ecstasy is weak, he exhibits ecstasy:[3] this "exhibition" is when that which he feels inwardly is manifested outwardly. If, however, his ecstasy is strong, he controls himself and is passive. God says: "Whereat the skins of those who fear their Lord do creep, then their skins and their hearts soften at the remembrance of God."[4] Al-Nūrī said: "Ecstasy is a flame which springs up in the secret heart, and appears out of longing, and at that visitation (*wārid*) the members are stirred either to joy or grief." They have said: "Ecstasy is akin to passing-away (*zawāl*), while gnosis is stable and does not pass away." The following verses are by Al-Junayd:

In ecstasy delighteth he
  Who finds in it his rest:
But when Truth cometh, ecstasy
  Itself is dispossessed.

Once ecstasy was my delight;
  But He Whom I did find
In ecstasy claims all my sight,
  And to the rest I'm blind.

[1] S. xxii. 45. [2] S. l. 36.

[3] The term *tawājud*, or "artificial ecstasy", is fully discussed and explained by Sarrāj in his *Kitāb al-Luma'*, pp. 301 ff. See Nicholson's summary, pp. 78 f.

[4] S. xxxix. 24.

One of the great Ṣūfīs composed the following:

He showed the veil, and its authority
Outswayed the might of all reality
And every imaged form. Alas, that He
Should ever be perceived in ecstasy,
Whereof the flame is but the imagery
Of a defeated incapacity.[1]
Ecstasy touches but the forms, which flee
Before His radiant divinity,
And it with them. I, too, found formerly
Delight in ecstasy; but, woe is me,
Now here I was, now there. Then, to my glee,
He granted me an attestation, free
Of all but the Attested: ecstasy
Was swallowed up, and every memory
Of visual form, in the one Unity.

One of the Ṣūfīs said: "Ecstasy is the glad tidings sent by God of the mystic's promotion to the stations of His contemplation." Another said:

It were more meet that He
Who with such bounty brought me ecstasy
Should of His boundless grace
Sweep clean my spirit of its every trace.

When first He came to me,
When first He stirred my soul to ecstasy,
I knew that He would bring
Gifts far beyond the mind's imagining.[2]

Al-Shiblī wrote the following:

I hold that ecstasy is doubt
If it spring not of witnessing:
And every witness is cast out,
When Truth its witness clear doth bring.

[1] That is, an inability to attain the higher state in which ecstasy disappears.
[2] Sc. the destroying of ecstasy.

Chapter LIV

THEIR DOCTRINE OF OVERMASTERY

Overmastery is a state experienced by the mystic, during which he is incapable of observing cause or preserving manner,[1] and entirely unable to discriminate concerning what comes upon him: he may even commit something which will earn him the disapprobation of those who do not understand his condition. When, however, the overmastering forces have subsided, he returns to his normal self. These forces may consist either of fear, awe, reverence, shame, or the like. An illustration is provided by the story of Abū Lubābah[2] ibn Mundhir. The Banū Qurayẓah wished to consult him, when the Prophet required them to submit to the authority of Sa'd ibn Mu'ādh: and he pointed with his hand to his throat, implying slaughter. Then he repented of what he had done, realising that he had been unfaithful to God and His Apostle: and he went away distracted, and finally tied himself up to one of the pillars of the mosque, saying: "I will not leave my place here until God forgives me for what I have done." He did this because of the fear of God which overmastered him, and prevented him from going to the Prophet as he should have done, according to God's command: "And if they, when they have wronged themselves, come to thee and ask pardon of God, and the Apostle asks pardon for them...."[3] For it is nowhere prescribed in the Law that a man shall be tied to a wall or a pillar. When the Prophet remarked how long he was in coming to him, he said: "If he had come to me, I would have asked pardon for him: but since he has done what he has done, I am not the one to set

[1] *Adab*, correct bearing towards God.

[2] This narrative is taken word for word from Ibn Hishām (*vide* Wüstenfeld's edition, p. 686).

[3] S. iv. 67.

him free from his place, until God forgives him."[1] When God saw that he was sincere, and that what had happened was the consequence of an overmastering fear, He forgave him. Then God revealed His forgiveness, and the Prophet set him free.[2] Now when this fear overmastered Abū Lubābah, he was incapable of observing the cause, to wit, that the Apostle should ask pardon, as God says: "And if they, when they have wronged themselves...." He was also incapable of preserving manner, namely, to excuse himself before him against whom he sinned, to wit, the Prophet. Similarly, 'Umar was overmastered by his zeal for the faith, so that he opposed the Prophet when he desired to make a truce with the infidels in the year of Al-Ḥudaybiyah:[3] 'Umar leapt up, and came to Abū Bakr, and said, "O Abū Bakr! is he not the Messenger of God?" He said, "Yes." 'Umar said, "Are we not Muslims?" He said, "Yes." 'Umar said, "Are they not infidels?" He said, "Yes." 'Umar said: "Then why do we bring worldly considerations into our religion?" Abū Bakr said: "O 'Umar! do thou cleave to his stirrup,[4] for I bear witness that he is God's Messenger." 'Umar said: "And I also bear witness that he is God's Messenger." Then he was overmastered by his feelings, and he came to the Prophet, and said to him just as he had said to Abū Bakr; and the Prophet answered him as Abū Bakr had done, and ended, "I am the servant of God and His Apostle: I will not oppose His command, and He will not abandon me." Thereafter 'Umar used to say: "I have not ceased to fast, to give alms, to set captives free, and to pray, in expiation of what I did that day, for I was afraid of the words which I had uttered: until at last I hoped that all was well." Similarly he opposed

[1] Ibn Hishām, p. 687.

[2] The exegesis which follows is omitted in some MSS.

[3] The narrative is copied from Ibn Hishām: *vide* Wüstenfeld's edition, p. 747. [4] Sc. obey his command.

the Prophet, when he prayed for 'Abdullāh ibn Ubayy.[1] 'Umar said: "Some change came over me, and I stood on his chest, and said, 'O Messenger of God! wilt thou pray for this man, seeing that he said such and such on such and such a day?'" So he enumerated the days, until the Prophet said to him: "Let me be: I have been given the choice, and I have chosen." So he prayed over him. 'Umar adds: "And I was astonished[2] at myself, and my boldness towards the Prophet." Another such story is that of Abū Ṭaybah,[3] who cupped the Prophet and then drank his blood, a thing prohibited by the Law: this he did in the state of being overmastered. The Prophet forgave him, however, saying, "Thou hast hedged thyself about with the fences of Hell."

Such stories as these—and there are many—prove that overmastering is a genuine state of the soul, during which it is permissible to do things not allowed in the state of repose. If, however, as in the case of Abū Bakr, a man is quiet even in this state, because of some higher condition, he will be more steady, and his state is more perfect.

Chapter LV

THEIR DOCTRINE OF INTOXICATION

Intoxication is evident when a man, while not being entirely unconscious to the things about him, is nevertheless unable to discriminate between them: that is, he is unable to distinguish between what is agreeable and pleasant, and what is the reverse, because of his association with God. The overmastering sense of God's being destroys his capacity to distinguish between what

[1] Again quoted from Ibn Hishām, p. 927.
[2] So Ibn Hishām: Kalābādhī reads "he was astonished at me".
[3] *Vide* Dhahabī, *al-Mushtabih* (ed. de Jong), p. 326.

pains him and what gives him pleasure. This is illustrated by certain narratives. There is, for example, the tradition of Ḥārithah, who said: "Equal in my sight are its stone and its clay, its gold and its silver." So 'Abdullāh ibn Mas'ūd said: "I do not care into which of the two states I may fall, whether it be wealth or poverty: for let it be poverty, then I may be patient, or let it be wealth, I will be grateful." He had lost all discrimination between the more congenial and its reverse, for he was overmastered by a sense of what he owed to God, namely, patience and gratitude.

Sobriety, which follows drunkenness, is a state in which a man can discriminate, and knows what is painful from what is pleasant, but deliberately chooses the former, if it be in accordance with God's will: then he feels no pain, but rather pleasure, in his painful experience. It is said that one of the great Ṣūfīs exclaimed: "If Thou[1] shouldst cut me up with affliction piece by piece, I should only feel towards Thee the greater love on love." Abu 'l-Dardā is related to have said: "I love death, for I long for my Lord; I love sickness, for then I may reflect on my sins; I love poverty, for I am submissive to my Lord." One of the Companions said: "How dear are the two detested things, death and poverty!" This state is more perfect (than the preceding), for the intoxicated man falls into what is hateful without being aware of it, so that he has no consciousness of a feeling of repulsion; whereas the other prefers pain to pleasure, and then finds pleasure in what pains him, for he is overwhelmed by the presence of Him who causes the pain. The sober man,[2] however, whose attribute is prior to the attribute of intoxication, will sometimes prefer pain to pleasure out of consideration of a reward or in expectation of a compensation: such a man feels pain in pain, and

[1] Reading with V.

[2] That is, the man who has not yet been intoxicated, as distinguished from the spiritually-sober.

pleasure in pleasure; his attributes are patience and gratitude.[1] One of the great Ṣūfīs composed these verses:

If, being sober, I
No more descry
Save what is His, what higher truths await
In drunkenness, which is the nobler state?

Now come sobriety,
Or let me be
Intoxicated; work out Thy design:
Drunken or sober, I am ever Thine.

He means that, if the state of discrimination even causes me to be aware only of what is God's,[2] and to lose sense of what is mine, what will the state of intoxication be like, a state in which discrimination passes away? It is God Who controls me in the discharge of my duties, and watches over me in my states. These two states have effect in me, but they really belong to God, and not to me at all: and I continue for ever in these two states.

Chapter LVI

THEIR DOCTRINE OF ABSENCE AND PRESENCE

Absence signifies that a man is unconscious of his own passions, and is not aware of them at all, although those passions still persist in him, only he is absent from them because he is present with what belongs to God. A man said to Al-Awzā'ī: "We saw your blue-eyed handmaid in the market." He replied: "Is she blue-eyed?" When Abū Sulayman al-Dārānī was told this story, he said: "The eyes of their hearts were opened, and the eyes of their heads were closed." So he points out that,

[1] Reading with Q.V.: the sober man is patient because he feels pain, and grateful because he feels pleasure.

[2] Reading with Q.V.

though he was unconscious of the fact that she was blue-eyed, nevertheless there persisted in him a delight in dark-eyed maidens, for he said: "Is she blue-eyed?"

Presence signifies that a man regards his passions as belonging to God, not to himself: whatever he may indulge in, he indulges in it in the spirit of servanthood and the submission of his human nature, not for the sake of pleasure or lust.

There is yet a second absence beyond this, in which a man is unconscious of his passing-away: there is no difference between the man who passes away in the presence of persistence, and the man who persists, as Ḥāriṯhah explained in his own case. Presence is a consciousness of being overwhelmed, not a visual consciousness: while absence is an absence of consciousness of what is profitable or harmful, not an absence consisting of being veiled and shrouded.[1] Al-Nūrī wrote:

> If I am present, no regard I see
> When I regard: it is enough that He
> Who, though unseen, is present everywhere,
> Doth hold my spirit's eye unceasingly.
>
> If I am absent—mystery how strange!—
> Absence through absence absently doth range:
> Then is His absence in a radiance fair
> Made manifest beyond all power of change.[2]

One of our Shaykhs explained presence as follows: "Presence means that, whatever one may witness, one is contemptuous of it, and it is as if non-existent, because of the overwhelming presence of God." This is the sense of the verses:

> Truly, all things but God are vain and void,
> And every loveliness must be destroyed.

So Moses said: "This is naught but Thy trial":[3] he

[1] This seems to be an attempt to elucidate the thesis that *fanā* and *baqā* are in essence identical.

[2] The commentator admits that he finds it hard to understand these verses: I do not contradict him.

[3] S. vii. 154.

considered the Samaritan as non-existent because of his consciousness of God. Al-Nūrī wrote:

God sent distracting cares to cover me,
And I am hid from all humanity:
His power unconfined
Dismays th' appraising mind.

Time knows not that I have in it no share,
And of time's chances I am unaware.
On God's command I wait,
And scorn the hand of fate.

Chapter LVII

THEIR DOCTRINE OF CONCENTRATION AND SEPARATION

The first part of concentration is the concentration of resolution, that is, that all one's resolves shall be a single resolve. So the Tradition runs: "If a man makes his resolves a single resolve, the resolve after the future state, God will suffice him for all his resolves: but if his resolves are divided, God does not care in which of their valleys he perishes." This is the state of endeavour and discipline. The concentration, however, which is the particular intention of the mystics is in fact a spiritual state: in this state the resolves are no longer separated, that the mystic must make a personal effort to concentrate them, but they are already concentrated, and become a single resolve in the presence of Him Who is their concentrator, so that the concentration which supervenes is solely through God, and none other.

The separation which follows concentration is a state in which the mystic is separated from his carnal resolves, and from the desire for pleasant and pleasurable things: he is separated from himself, and his motions are no longer for himself. It may happen in certain states that the concentrated man will regard his own desires, and not be prevented from doing so: but he is not able to gratify them, and they have no influence on him; and he does not object to this, but rather desires it, for he knows that this is God's doing, and that God thus chooses him and draws him to Himself.

One of the great Ṣūfīs was asked, "What is concentration?" He replied: "It is the concentration of the innermost heart on that which is indispensable, and its subjection therein: for He has neither like nor opposite." Another said: "He concentrated them on Himself when He joined them through the renouncing of it,[1] and He separated them from Himself when they sought Him through what was of themselves: dissolution occurred because of the desire for secondary causes, and concentration resulted when they contemplated Him in every matter."[2] The separation of which he speaks is that which comes before concentration: he means that separation is the outcome of seeking to come near to God through works, whereas when they see that it is God that brings them near, then they attain concentration. One of the great Ṣūfīs wrote:

By concentration they are raised sublime
From selfhood, as before the birth of time,
And separation gives them leave to be,
But for a while, but unsubstantially.
Lost to themselves, uprooted from mankind,
An attestation of the Truth they find:
In concentration free of time they range
Beyond this pathless wilderness of change.
As, ere time was, unformed, inanimate,
They had not seen, that they should concentrate;
Then, being separated, they were given
That ampler life, which once was theirs in heaven:
So absence is the fruit of concentration,
And presence the reward of separation.
Upon these twain, to be or not to be
Hangs on the thread of relativity.

[1] Probably referring to a subject previously expressed, such as "otherness".
[2] Lit. "in every chapter".

The words "by concentration they are raised sublime from selfhood" mean, that their knowledge that they exist for God in His knowledge of them caused them to lose themselves during the period when they came to exist for Him: so concentration produced the state of non-existence, inasmuch as nothing existed save God's knowledge of them. Separation is the condition of their being brought out of non-existence into existence. The words "lost to themselves" mean, that they regard themselves, during the time of their existence, as they were when they lacked (existence), having no power either to harm or to profit, while God's knowledge does not change in them. Their concentration is that God effaces them from the attributes of unreal form (*rasm*), that is to say, their acts and attributes, inasmuch as these do not possess the power to effect change or alteration, but are in accordance with God's knowledge, predestining and decree. Their condition of existence was annihilated in God's eternal knowledge, for they were non-existent, possessing neither existence nor form. When God brought them into existence, then, He merely effected in them that which He had previously intended for them. Concentration means, that they are absent from being present (in this world), and from regarding themselves as self-determining, while separation means that they regard their own states and acts. Being and not-being are conditions which alternate in them, but not in God.[1]

Abū Sa'īd al-Kharrāz said: "Concentration means, that God caused them to discover Himself in themselves, or rather He abolished their existence for themselves on their coming to exist for Him." His intention is the same as that of the Tradition: "I am for him hearing, sight and hand, so that through Me he hears, and through Me he sees."[2] This is because formerly

[1] The paragraph which follows is not contained in some MSS., and may be spurious.

[2] For the full text, *vide* Makkī, *Qūt al-qulūb*, II, p. 67; cf. Massignon, *Essai*, p. 107.

they conducted their affairs through themselves and for themselves,[1] whereas now they conduct their affairs for God and through God.

Chapter LVIII

THEIR DOCTRINE OF REVELATION AND VEILING

Sahl said: "Revelation is in three states: revelation of an essence, which is unveiling; revelation of the qualities of essence, which is illumination; and revelation of the condition of essence, which is the life of the world to come." His words "revelation of an essence, which is unveiling" imply that revealing of overmastery which occurs in this world, as illustrated by the saying of 'Abdullāh ibn 'Umar, "We saw God in that place", that is, during the procession of the Kaaba[2]—(so the Prophet said: "Worship God as if thou seest Him")—and the visual revealing which occurs in the world to come. By "revelation of the qualities of essence, which is illumination" he means, that God's power over him is revealed to him, so that he fears none but God, together with God's sufficiency for him, so that he hopes of none but God: a condition exemplified as appertaining to all the qualities of essence by the saying of Ḥāri<u>th</u>ah, "It was as though I beheld the Throne of my Lord coming forth"; it was as though God's speech was revealed to him during His communicating, so that the communication became for him as it were a direct vision. As for the revelation of the condition, this will come in the next world, "a part in Paradise and a part in the blaze".[3]

One of the great Ṣūfīs said: "The sign of God's

[1] Omitting the negative, which appears a misreading.
[2] Cf. p. 119.
[3] S. xlii. 5.

revelation to the heart is, that the heart does not attest that which expression can master or understanding contain: if a man expresses or understands, then it is a thought of indication, not a regard of veneration".[1] He means that (with revelation) he attests what cannot be expressed, because his attesting is in the spirit of veneration and awe, and this makes it impossible for him to elucidate his attestation. One of the Ṣūfīs composed the following:

> When Truth its light doth show,
> I lose myself in reverence,
> And am as one who never travelled thence
> To life below.
>
> When I am absented
> From self in Him, and Him attain,
> Attainment's self thereafter proveth vain,
> And self is dead.
>
> In union divine
> With Him, Him only I do see:
> I dwell alone, and that felicity
> No more is mine.
>
> This mystic union
> From self hath separated me:
> Now witness concentration's mystery
> Of two made one.

This is the meaning: when truth appears, reverence overpowers me, so that I am absent in the attestation of reverence from the capacity of communicating (my experience), so that I am as one to whom God never appeared. When I am absent from myself, then my existence is His, and when I am absent, my (personal) existence is lost. The condition of union, which is my passing away from self, does not allow me to witness any but Him; while the condition of detachment, and of persisting in my own attribute, makes me absent

[1] This means, that if expression is possible, then the mystic is experiencing not the direct vision of God's essence which is accompanied with veneration, but the intellectual proof which is the result of thought.

from witnessing Him. It is therefore as if my concentration through Him separates me from myself. The condition of union means, that God controls me, not I myself, in my actions; for God exists, not I. So God said to His Prophet: "Nor didst thou shoot when thou didst shoot, but God did shoot".[1] This is the expression of mystical feeling:[2] theology teaches that God is my controller, and I through Him control myself, so that there is both Served and servant. One of the Ṣūfīs said: "Revelation is the raising of the veils of creaturehood, not that any change transpires in God's essence: veiling means that creaturehood prevents thee from seeing the unseen." By "the raising of the veils of creaturehood" he means that God sustains thee during the inflow of revelation of the unseen, for creaturehood cannot withstand the states that belong to the unseen. The veiling which comes after revelation is that state in which things are veiled from thee, so that thou dost not attest them: this is illustrated by the story of 'Abdullāh ibn 'Umar. He was engaged in circumambulating the Kaaba, when a man saluted him. He did not answer him; and when the man complained of this, he said, "We were beholding God in that place." Of God's revelation to him he gave evidence by saying, "We were beholding God", while of his veiling he gave evidence by being unconscious of the other man greeting him. As one of the great Ṣūfīs has said:

> God's secrets to the veiled are not revealed;
> Seek not to publish what He hath concealed
> From thee: with what thou canst not comprehend
> To occupy thyself do not pretend.
> It is not seemly that Reality,
> Being manifest, should hide itself in thee.

[1] S. viii. 17.

[2] To avoid the implication of *ḥulūl*: the identity of man and God is a mystical experience; in reality they still remain God and man.

Chapter LIX

THEIR DOCTRINE OF PASSING-AWAY AND PERSISTENCE

Passing-away is a state in which all passions pass away, so that the mystic experiences no feelings towards anything whatsoever, and loses all sense of discrimination: he has passed away from all things, and is wholly absorbed with that through which he has passed away. So 'Āmir ibn 'Abdillāh said: "I do not care whether I saw a woman or a wall." Then God Himself undertakes to control him, and controls him so that he performs his duties to God, and accords with His will: he is wholly preserved in paying God His due, and is withdrawn from all personal interests and from all opposition to God, so that he has not even the means to oppose Him. This is what is meant by divine protection (*'iṣmah*), and it is this to which the famous Tradition refers, "I am for him hearing and sight."[1]

Persistence, which follows passing-away, means that the mystic passes away from what belongs to himself, and persists through what is God's. One of the great Ṣūfīs said: "Persistence is the station of the prophets." They were clad in the peace of God (*sakīnah*), and whatever comes to them cannot prevent them from doing their duty to God, and receiving His bounty; for "that is God's grace; He gives it unto whom He pleases".[2] When a man persists, all things become for him but one thing, and his every motion is in accord, not in disaccord, with God: he passes away from disaccord, and persists in accord. Now the fact that "all things become for him but one thing" does not imply

[1] *Vide* p. 116, *supra.*
[2] S. v. 59.

that disaccord is in him accord, or that prohibition is for him the same as commandment:[1] it means simply that whatever occurs to him occurs in agreement with God's command and pleasure, nothing that displeases God. What he does, he does unto God, not for his own pleasure, whether in this world or the next. This is what is meant by the Ṣūfī expression, "he passes away from his own attributes and persists in the attributes of God": for what God does, He does for another, not for Himself, neither seeking thereby to derive an advantage, nor intending to ward off harm—God is far removed from that!—but solely in order either to benefit or to harm others. Similarly, the mystic who persists through God, and passes away from self, does what he does not to derive personal advantage or to ward off from himself any harm, but simply without any intention by his act either to derive advantage or to ward off harm. All personal feelings and the desire for personal advantage have ceased in him. Now this only refers to purpose and intention: it must not be understood to imply that the mystic experiences no pleasure at all in performing his duty to God, but rather that he does it unto God, not out of any desire for reward or fear of punishment. It is true that these two feelings, desire and fear, continue to persist in him: but he desires the reward of God in order to accord with God, for God has desired this for him, and has commanded him to ask this of Him, and so he does not act for his own pleasure; similarly he fears God's punishment, for he reveres God and would accord with Him, and God has caused His creatures to fear;[2] so in all his motions he acts for the sake of

[1] This gives the answer to the excesses of the Malāmatīyah, who held that the mystic cannot sin, and may even deliberately do things contrary to God's will, in order to court men's disapproval.

[2] Some MSS. add: "and He desires him to fear His punishment, so that he fears His punishment for that reason, not because of the pain (it may bring)."

another's pleasure, not for his own. In this sense the saying is to be understood: "The believer eats at the appetite of his family." One of the Ṣūfīs composed these lines:

From self and selfhood's strangling chain
God set him free; and then again
Clothed him in unsubstantial clay,
That he God's mysteries might display.

So form from form must be withdrawn
At revelation's dazzling dawn:
God's sure and omnipresent will
Shall every heart with rapture fill.

The whole meaning of passing-away and persistence is, therefore, that the mystic passes away from his own feelings, and persists in the feelings of another.

There is also another kind of passing-away, which consists in passing away from the very consciousness of disaccord (with God), and from all motions deliberately aimed at disaccord, and in persisting consciously in accord (with God), deliberately and actually aiming at this in all motions. In this there is also a passing-away from respecting what is other than God, and persistence in respecting God. This latter meaning is exemplified by the story of Abū Ḥāzim. He said: "What is this world? As for what is past, that is dreams; and as for what remains, that is vain hopes and delusion. And what is Satan, that he should be feared? If he is obeyed, he cannot benefit, and if he is disobeyed, he cannot harm." He was as though neither this world nor Satan existed for him. The passing-away from personal feelings is illustrated by the story of 'Abdullāh ibn Mas'ūd, who said: "I did not know that any of Muḥammad's companions desired this world, until God said, 'Amongst you are those who love this world, and amongst you are those who love the next'."[1] He had passed away from the desire for this world. To this variety also belongs the saying of Ḥārithah:

[1] S. iii. 146.

"I turned myself away from this world, and it is as if I behold the Throne of my Lord coming forth." He had passed away from the temporal into the eternal, and from all other into the All-Powerful. Similar is the story of 'Abdullāh ibn 'Umar. A man greeted him while he was circumambulating the Kaaba, and he did not answer him. The man complained of this to some of his friends; and 'Abdullāh said: "We were beholding God in that place." Similar also is the saying of 'Āmir ibn 'Abd al-Qays: "I would rather be run through with spear-heads one after another, than experience what you mention"—that is, during prayer.[1] Thereupon Al-Ḥasan said: "The like of this man God hath not chosen among us." There is a further passing-away, which consists in being entirely unconscious of external things, as was the case with Moses, when God made revelation to the mountain, "and Moses fell down in a swoon":[2] and in his second state,[3] he was unable to explain his former state, nor did He Who caused him to be unconscious inform him thereof.

Abū Sa'īd al-Kharrāz said: "The sign of the mystic's passing-away is the departing of his desire of this world and the next, except his desire of God. Then there appears to him a revelation of God's power, and shows him his desire of God departing in reverence to God; then there appears to him a revelation of God, and shows him the departing of his desire of the vision of the departing of his desire; and there remains the vision of what was of God for God, and the One and Eternal is alone in His Oneness; and with God there is not for other than God either passing-away or persistence." The words "departing of his desire of this world" mean the quest for material things, and "the next" the

[1] The story is, that certain men were discussing what thoughts occurred to them when they were praying. This was 'Āmir's comment.

[2] S. vii. 139.

[3] That is, when he recovered.

quest for compensations. His "desire of God" remains, for that is God's pleasure with him and nearness to Him.[1] Then there comes upon him a condition of reverence for God, that He should come near or be pleased with the like of him: so he despises himself, and reveres God. Finally there comes upon him a condition in which God's right entirely swallows him up, and makes him unconscious of the vision of his own attribute, that is, the vision of the departing of his desire. There then remains in him only what proceeds from God to him, and what proceeds from him to God passes away from him. So he becomes as he was when he existed in God's knowledge, before God brought him into being, and when that which came to him from God came without any act on his part.

Passing-away may be expressed in another way. Passing-away is being absent from human qualities in (undertaking) the fearful burden[2] of the divine qualities so that the human qualities of ignorance and injustice pass away, as God says: "But man bore it: verily, he is ever unjust and ignorant."[3] These qualities also include ingratitude, thanklessness, and every blameworthy attribute: and this all passes away, in the sense that God's knowledge prevails over man's ignorance, God's justice over man's injustice, God's gratitude over man's ingratitude, and so on. Abu 'l-Qāsim Fāris said: "Passing-away is the state of one who does not witness his own attribute, but rather witnesses it as being concealed by Him Who causes it to be absent." He also said: "The passing-away of human attributes is not to be understood as meaning that they do not exist, but rather that they are covered by a pleasure which supplants the

[1] This could read "his pleasure in God", etc.; but the words which follow militate against this interpretation.

[2] Sc. the burden referred to in the quotation which follows: the burden of the faith, which the heavens and earth refused to bear.

[3] S. xxxiii. 72.

realisation of pain." This pleasure which comes to the mystic in his spiritual state is like that which befel the women-companions of Joseph: "they cut their hands"[1] because their own attributes had passed away, and because the joy which came into their hearts when they looked upon Joseph made them unconscious of the pain they suffered in cutting their hands. On this matter one of our contemporaries has composed the following poem:

When Egypt's women cut their hands
  Because a human form was fair,
They knew the rapture that withstands
  All shocks, and felt no anguish there.

To every human quality
  Of pleasure or displeasure dead,
And from all attributes set free,
  They heeded not their palms that bled.

But she who was the prince's wife
  Cut not her hands, nor let them bleed:
For Joseph was her love and life,
  And Joseph shared not in that deed.[2]

The following verses also illustrate the state of passing-away:[3]

So we remembered—yet oblivion
Was not our habit: but a radiance shone,
A magical breeze breathed, and God was near.
Then vanished selfhood utterly, and I
Remained His only, Who with tidings clear
Attests His Being, and is known thereby.

Certain of the Ṣūfīs count these states as a single state, in spite of the fact that various terms are applied to them. Thus they equate passing-away and con-

[1] S. xii. 31.

[2] The last verse means, that as the wife of Potiphar was completely absorbed in Joseph, her actions could not be other than his: and he did not cut his hands. This is an interesting early example of the spiritualising of a theme which later became a favourite meditation of the mystical poets of Persia.

[3] These verses are quoted earlier in the book, cf. *supra*, p. 97.

tinuance, concentration and separation, and similarly absence and presence, intoxication and sobriety. For the mystic passes away from what belongs to himself, and persists through what belongs to God: while conversely he persists through what belongs to God, and so passes away from what belongs to himself. When he passes away, he is also concentrated, because he only witnesses God: when he is concentrated, he is also separated, for he does not witness himself, nor his fellows. He persists because he abides with God, Who concentrates him on Himself; he passes away from other than God, because he is separated therefrom. He is absent and intoxicated, because the power of discrimination—which we have explained in connection with pleasures and pains—passes away, and in this sense all things become one to him. He does not attest the phenomenon of disaccord, for God only suffers him to act in accord with Himself. Discrimination can only occur with reference to two things: and when all things have become a single thing, it naturally follows that discrimination is at an end.

Another group explain passing-away as follows: the mystic is removed from every personal trace (*rasm*), and from all such trace without him (*marsūm*), so that during his mystical moment (*waqt*) he remains without persistence so far as he knows, without passing-away so far as he is conscious, and without moment, so far as he can understand; rather, it is his Creator Who knows of his persistence and passing-away, and He preserves him from every blameworthy act.

They are at variance as to whether the mystic who has once passed away ever returns to remain in his own attributes. Some say that the mystic does so return, and that the condition of passing-away is not permanent: for if it were so, then the mystic's members would necessarily be useless for performing religious duties, and indeed would be incapable of doing a single thing connected with his life in this world as well as in the next.[1] In this connection Abu 'l-'Abbās ibn 'Aṭā has written a book, entitled "The return and the origin of the attributes." The great Ṣūfīs, however, and those who have had true experience, among them Al-Junayd, Al-Kharrāz and Al-Nūrī, do not hold that the mystic returns to his own attributes after passing away. They argue that passing-away is a divine bounty and gift to the mystic, a special mark of favour, not an acquired condition:[2] it is a thing which God vouchsafes to those whom He has chosen and elected for Himself. Therefore, if He were to return the mystic to his own attribute, He would be taking away what He had given, and recalling what He had accorded, and this would not be at all in keeping with God's nature; or if it be regarded as due to a change of mind,[3] that is a characteristic of one who gains further knowledge, and this is denied in the case of God; or if it be interpreted as a trick or a deceit, God cannot be called a trickster, and He does not deceive the believers, He only deceives hypocrites and unbelievers. Passing-away is not a station which may be attained by personal merit, that its opposite[4] should also be thus acquired.

If it be objected that the mystic then turns away from faith, which is the noblest of ranks, for by it all the stations are attained, this is our answer. The faith from which a man may turn back is a faith which he has acquired by his tongue's confession and the work of his members: such a faith does not mingle in his real heart, either as a direct realisation, or as a true belief. He merely professes, without knowing the truth of what he professes: as the Tradition runs, "The angel (of death) will come to a man when he is set in his

[1] That is, he is unable to earn a livelihood so as to remain in this world, and equally unable to perform his religious duties so as to be fitted for the world to come.

[2] A condition which is the result of previous actions.

[3] That is, God first thought that this mystic deserved such a gift, and then, on learning more about him, changed His mind.

[4] Sc. *baqā*.

grave, and will say, 'What sayest thou of this man?' And he will say, 'I heard other men saying a certain thing, and so I said it'." Such a man is a doubter, and has no certainty. Or else he confesses with his tongue, but secretly belies his confession: so the hypocrite confesses with his tongue, and in his heart belies his confession, secretly opposing it. Or haply he confesses with his tongue, and does not belie his confession in his heart, nor secretly opposes it, but what he confesses has no soundness in it, either acquired or inspired: he has not acquired its verification through science, that he may have proofs of its soundness, and he has not experienced in his heart a spiritual condition putting an end to all his doubts. Whatever his case may be, unhappiness is his predestined portion from God: doubts occur to him, inspired either by his own thoughts or the disputations of another; he is tempted, and converted from faith to its opposite. As for the man to whom God has allotted the better portion, no doubts occur to him, and all objections leave him: either as the result of what he has acquired from the knowledge of the Book and the Sunna, and intellectual proofs, which ends all evil thoughts and repulses all doubts of disputation, since it is not possible for a thing which is true to be opposed by proofs which are also true, and so no doubts occur to him at all; or else because he has been granted a sound faith, and God Himself repulses from him all evil thoughts by His protection, and likewise repulses from him the disputer that raises doubts by His special bounty, so that he no more faces him, and then the soundness of his faith is secure, even though he may not possess the power of exposition necessary to make dispute with the disputer, or to dispel his own thoughts; or else because the soundness of his profession has been assured by vision or revelation, as was the case with Ḥārit͟hah, who tells us that he actually saw what he believed in, so that that which was (normally) absent took the place of what was present, for he says that he turned away from the seen world, and the unseen became for him seen, and the seen unseen—so Al-Dārānī says, "The eyes of their hearts were opened, and the eyes of their heads were closed."

When a man's profession is made sound in this way, he does not return from the next world to this world, or leave what is better for what is worse. All this is the means by which God's protection operates, and it is the verification of His promise: "God answers those who believe with the sure word in this world's life and in the next."[1] It is therefore established that the true believer cannot be moved from his faith, because this faith is God's special bounty and gift and favour to him: far be it from God to take back what He has given, or to recall what He has bestowed.

Now faith which is true, and faith which is merely formal, have outwardly the same appearance, but their real natures are diverse: on the other hand, passing-away, and all the other special stations, are outwardly diverse, but their true natures are the same.[2] They do not come as a result of personal merit, but as a (divine) favour.[3] Hence it is absurd to maintain that the mystic who has passed away returns to his own attributes. If a man holds this view, while asserting that God first chooses and elects the mystic for Himself, and then restores him, it is as if he is saying that God chooses what He does not in reality choose, and elects what He does not elect. This, of course, is absurd: and to say that it is possible in order to train the mystic and to preserve him from temptation is equally absurd, for God does not preserve in His servant what He has given him in order to take it away again, or to restore

[1] S. xiv. 32.

[2] Returning to the argument above, that all these higher stations are identical.

[3] According to the Ṣūfī doctrine that the *maqām* is the result of personal effort, but the *ḥāl* is a divinely-accorded favour.

him from a higher station to a lower. This is illustrated in the case of the prophets: for such a view as the foregoing would imply that it is possible for God[1] to preserve the prophets from the occasions of being tempted, so restoring them from the rank of prophets to that of saints or even lower; and that is absurd. God's favours in protecting His prophets from sin, and preserving His saints from temptation, are too many to be numbered or reckoned, and His power is too great to be confined to one act rather than another.

If an objection be made that the case of him to whom God brought His signs, "and who stepped away therefrom",[2] opposes this view, the objection is not valid. The man who "stepped away" had never enjoyed any spiritual state, or experienced any station, and he was never chosen or elected (by God): rather, he was being brought gradually to destruction, for he was deceived and deluded. He was outwardly marked with the signs of the elect, but in reality he was of the rejected: he was outwardly adorned with seemly occupations and pure litanies, but he was blind of heart and veiled of conscience. He had never known the savour of election, nor tasted the pleasure of faith, and he had never known God after the manner of sensing His presence (*s͟hubūd*): and so God indicated when He said, "and he was one of the beguiled".[2] Similarly God said of Iblīs: "And he became one of the misbelievers."[3] Al-Junayd said: "Iblīs never attained contemplation when he was obedient, and Adam never lost contemplation when he was disobedient." Abū Sulaymān said: "A man never turns back, save when he is on the road; if they had arrived, they would never have returned."[4]

[1] Omitting the negative with V.: the prophets were exposed to temptation, but because of the divine *'iṣmah* did not fall. The saints were not exposed to temptation.

[2] S. vii. 174.

[3] S. ii. 32.

[4] Supporting the thesis that the *fānī* does not return to his former state.

The mystic who has passed away is preserved in his duties to God, as is illustrated by the following story. A man said to Al-Junayd: "Abu 'l-Ḥusayn al-Nūrī has been standing in the S͟hūnīzī mosque for some days, without eating or drinking or sleeping, and all the time he says, 'God, God'; and he says his prayers at their proper times." Then someone said who was standing by: "He is sober."[1] Al-Junayd said: "No: the ecstatics are preserved before God during their ecstasies."

Now if the mystic who has passed away does return to any attributes at all, he does not return to his own, but he is placed in that station in which he persists through the attributes of God. The man who passes away is not swooning, or mad, nor do his human qualities disappear, that he should become an angel or a spirit: he merely passes away from the sense of his own feelings, as we have explained above.

The man who passes away may be of one of two kinds. He may be such as cannot be taken as a leader or a model: his passing-away may consist of being absent from his own attributes, so that he appears to be really mad and to have lost his reason, because he loses all discrimination as to what is to his advantage, and no longer seeks his own pleasure. For all that he is preserved to perform his duties to God. Of such men there have been many in the community, among them the Abyssinian Hilāl, who was a slave of Al-Mug͟hīrah ibn S͟hu'bah during the Prophet's lifetime, and whom the Prophet specially mentioned; Uways al-Qaranī, who lived in the days of 'Umar ibn al-K͟haṭṭāb, and whom the Prophet mentioned (aforehand) to 'Umar and 'Alī; and many others, down to 'Ulayyān the Mad and Sa'dūn and others. On the other hand, he may be a leader to be followed, governing those who attach themselves to him: such a man is appointed to govern and instruct his fellows. He is

[1] That is, he is not intoxicated at all, and does not experience ecstasy.

transferred to the condition of persistence, and he governs his affairs through the qualities of God, not through his own attributes, in the manner which we have previously mentioned. A man asked Junayd: "What is insight (*firāsah*)?" He replied: "It is the alighting of accuracy." The other said: "Does the man of insight possess this quality at the time of alighting, or at all times?" He answered: "At all times. It is a gift, and therefore it remains with him perpetually." So Al-Junayd implies that (divine) gifts remain perpetually.

If a man follows closely the books of the Ṣūfīs, and understands their references, he will know that their doctrine is as we have related. Indeed, this and similar questions are not documented or made into monographs by the Ṣūfīs: but this is known from the correct understanding of their enigmas and the true perception of their hints to be their true doctrine. God knows best.

Chapter LX

THEIR DOCTRINE OF THE REALITIES OF GNOSIS

One of the Shaykhs said: "Gnosis is of two kinds: the gnosis of a truth, and the gnosis of a reality. The gnosis of truth is the assertion of God's Unity over the attributes which He has put forth. As for the gnosis of reality, this is the gnosis that there is no means of reaching that gnosis, because the impermeable nature (of God) and the verification of (His) lordliness are impossible to comprehend: God says, 'But they do not comprehend knowledge of Him.'[1] The Impermeable is He the realities of Whose attributes and qualities cannot be perceived."

[1] S. xx. 109.

One of the great Ṣūfīs said: "Gnosis is the summoning of the heart through various kinds of meditation to observe the ecstasies induced by acts of recollection according to the successive signs of revelation." He means, that the heart so witnesses the power of God, and experiences the magnifying of His truth and the glorifying of His might, that expression thereof is impossible.

Al-Junayd was asked: "What is gnosis?" He replied: "It is the hovering of the heart between declaring God too great to be comprehended, and declaring Him too mighty to be perceived." He was asked another time the same question, and he replied: "It consists in knowing that, whatever may be imaged in thy heart, God is the opposite of it. Alas, for the bewilderment! God has no part in any man, and no man has any part in Him. He[1] is an existence that goes to and fro in non-existence. Expression is not prepared for Him: for the creature is preceded, and that which is preceded cannot comprehend that which precedes." The meaning of the words "He is an existence that goes to and fro in non-existence" is, the man who experiences this condition (is an existence, etc.): he (sc. Al-Junayd) says that he is existent to the eye and vision, but as if non-existent in attribute and quality. Al-Junayd also said: "Gnosis is the thought's witnessing of the issues of the return, and that the gnostic should have no power of either excess or shortcoming." He means, that the gnostic does not witness his own state, but only God's prevenient knowledge of him, and that his return[2] is to that which issued to him from God beforetime, and that he is controlled (by God) both in service and in shortcoming. One of the Ṣūfīs said: "When gnosis comes down into the heart, the heart has not the means

[1] As the commentator of V. points out, this pronoun appears, at any rate at first sight, to refer to God: Kalābādhī takes it to refer to the mystic, and explains the saying accordingly.

[2] Sc. to the next world after death.

to bear it: it is as the sun, whose rays prevent the beholder from perceiving its limit and essence." Ibn al-Farghānī said: "Who knows the form (*rasm*) is proud, who knows the impress (*wasm*) is bewildered,[1] who knows what has gone before is inert, who knows God is firm, and who knows the Overruler is humble." He means, that if a man attests himself performing his duties to God, he is vain; if he attests what God has issued for him beforetime, he is bewildered, because he does not know what is God's knowledge of him, or what the Pen inscribed concerning him; if he knows that what has been preordained for him to have cannot be advanced or retarded, he lacks the faculty to seek; if he knows God, and God's power over him, and that He is sufficient for him, he is firm, and is not perturbed by the things that terrify, or by his needs; and if he knows that God overrules his affairs, he humbles himself to God's judgment and decrees. One of the great Ṣūfīs said: "When God gives him the knowledge of Himself, He so stays his gnosis that he feels neither love, nor fear, nor hope, nor poverty, nor wealth; for all these are short of the goals, and God is beyond all ends." He means, that he does not feel these states, because they are his own attributes: and his attributes are too straitened to attain what God deserves thereof. The following verses are attributed to one of the great Ṣūfīs:

Thou art my guardian, Lord, and my defence,
Thou keep'st me from the noisome pestilence;
Thou art my plea before mine adversary,
And when I thirst, Thou satisfiest me.

The man of God takes horse, for he doth hope
To scale in secret heaven's highest slope:
Then, plunging headlong in the restless main,
Learns every marvel that its depths contain.[2]

[1] By *rasm* is meant the material, unreal impress; by *wasm* the divine, spiritual, real impress.

[2] As the commentator explains, the former is *malakūt*, the latter *mulk*: that world and this.

He breaks the seals of mysteries which impart
The elixir of every lover's heart;
But at the meeting[1] so amazed doth lie
That, being yet alive, he seems to die.

He means, that he is amazed and bewildered by the inward sense of reverence and awe of God which comes to him, so that when one looks at him, he appears, while yet living, to be dead: he passes away from the consideration of what is his, for he finds in himself no power of advancing or retarding (what God has ordained).

Chapter LXI

THEIR DOCTRINE OF UNIFICATION

Unification has seven elements: the isolation of the eternal from the temporal; the exalting of the Eternal above the perception of the created; giving up equating the attributes; abolishing the principle of causation from the attribute of Lordship; raising God above the power of the temporal to affect or change Him, and exalting Him above all (mental) discrimination and consideration; and declaring Him to be free of the principle of analogy.

Muḥammad ibn Mūsā al-Wāsiṭī said: "The sum of unification is this, that all the capacity of the tongue to utter, or of exposition to express, glorification or detachment or separation, is caused; and reality is beyond that." He means that all these belong to personal qualities and attributes, which, like the person, are originated and caused; while the reality of God is His qualification of Himself. One of the great Ṣūfīs said: "Unification is thy isolation as a single individual, and consists in God causing thee not to witness thyself."

[1] Sc. with God.

Fāris said: "Unification is not sound, so long as there remains with thee any connection of detachment. When unification is in speech, God does not see the unitarian's heart single in Him, and when unification is in state, the unitarian is absent from all speech: but the vision of God is a state which suffers the mystic to behold all that belongs to God. There is no other way, however, to God's unification, than by speech or state."[1] One of the Ṣūfīs said: "Unification consists in departing from thyself entirely, on the condition, however, of discharging fully all that is incumbent on thee, and that nothing should return to thee to sever thee from God." He means, that a man should make every effort to discharge his duty to God, and then free himself from considering the fact that he has discharged his duty: his unification discharges him from his own attributes, and nothing thereof returns to him, for such would sever him from God. Al-Shiblī said: "The mystic does not attain true unification, until he feels estranged from his own conscience, because God manifests to Him." Another said: "The unitarian is the man whom God has divided entirely from both worlds, for God defends His sanctuary, and He has said, 'We are your patrons in the life of this world and in the next':[2] therefore we do not restore thee to any being (*ma'nā*) other than us, in this world or the next. This is the mark of the unitarian: that there passes over him no recollection of the valuation of anything which possesses no reality before God. All attestations are turned away from his conscience, and all compensations driven out of his heart:[3] he beholds no attestation, serves no compensation, studies no secret, and

[1] That is, true unification is beyond speech and state: but the way to unification is only by speech or state.

[2] S. xxxi. 41.

[3] The "attestations" are the things of this world, the "compensations" the rewards which he hopes to obtain in the next world.

heeds no kindness.[1] While in (the performance of) his duty he is veiled from (the consideration that he has performed) his duty, and while subject to passion he is deprived of passion. He has no portion in any portion, for he is imprisoned in the amplest of all portions. God is the amplest of all portions: when he lacks God, he lacks everything, even though he may possess all phenomena; and when he finds God, he possesses everything, even though he may not own a single atom." The writer means, that while he is performing his duty he is veiled from seeing that he is performing his duty: he is also deprived of his passions, while he yet sees his soul executing its passions. His portion of God is the existence of God: he is imprisoned in it, and has no power of advancing or retarding. One of the Ṣūfīs wrote this verse:

So Truth is known in ecstasy,
For truth will everywhere prevail;
And even the greatest mind must fail
To comprehend this mystery.

Chapter LXII

THEIR DOCTRINE OF THE DESCRIPTION OF THE GNOSTIC

Al-Ḥasan ibn 'Alī ibn Yazdāniyār was asked: "When is the gnostic in the presence of God?" He replied: "When the Attestation appears, and the attestations pass away, the senses depart, and sincerity is abolished." When he says "the Attestation appears", he means the attestation of God, that is, what He did with the mystic aforetime, His kindness and bounteous gift of

[1] He "studies no secret" appears to mean that he pays no attention to his own heart; and "heeds no kindness" to mean that he is so absorbed in God the Beneficent that he has no thought for His benefactions.

gnosis, unification, and faith in Him: the consideration of this causes the mystic's own acts, his own piety and obedience, to pass away from his thoughts. He then sees the much that is of himself swallowed up in the little that is of God, even though what is of God is much, and what is of himself is little. The passing-away of attestations is the giving up of considering other men, as to whether they harm or profit, blame or praise: while the departing of the senses is exemplified by the Tradition, "through Me he speaks and through Me he sees".[1] The abolishing of sincerity means that, when the mystic considers his own quality—for his attributes are subject to causation like himself—he no longer considers himself as sincere, and he no longer thinks that his actions have ever been or will ever be sincere.

Dhu 'l-Nūn was asked: "What is the end of the gnostic?" He answered: "When he is as he was where he was before he was." He meant, that he contemplates God and His actions rather than contemplating himself and his own actions. Another said: "The man who knows God best is the most violently bewildered." Dhu 'l-Nūn was asked: "What is the first step the gnostic must surmount?" He replied: "Bewilderment; then need, then union, then bewilderment." The first bewilderment is at God's acts and bounties towards him: for he sees that his gratitude is not equal to God's bounties, and he knows that he is required to be grateful for them; even if he is grateful, his gratitude is a bounty for which he must be grateful. He feels that his acts are not worthy for him to meet God with: for he makes little of them, accounting them to be incumbent on him, and not under any circumstances to be omitted. It is said that Al-Shiblī on one occasion stood up to pray, and waited a long time, and then prayed; and when he had finished his prayer, he said: "Alas! if I pray, I deny, and if I do not pray, I am ungrateful." He

[1] Cf. p. 116, n. 2.

meant: I deny the magnitude of the favour and the perfection of the bounty, when I compare that with my own miserable act of gratitude. Then he began to recite:

Now praised be God, that like a frog am I
Whose sustenance the watery deeps supply.
It opes its mouth, and straightway it is filled;
It holds its peace, and must in sorrow die.

The second bewilderment is in the pathless wildernesses of unification, in which the gnostic's understanding is lost, and his intellect shrinks, before the greatness of God's power and awe and majesty. It has been said: "This side of unification there are wildernesses in which the thoughts are lost." Abu 'l-Sawdā asked one of the great Ṣūfīs: "Does the gnostic possess an occasion (*waqt*)?" He replied: "No." The other asked: "Why not?" The Ṣūfī answered: "Because the occasion is an interval for refreshment after anguish, and gnosis is (like) waves which choke (the gnostic), now raising him up, now dashing him down, and his occasion is black and dark."[1] Then he said:

Gnosis makes one demand, and only one:
That everything from thee shall be effaced.
So, when the long research was first begun,
The seeker learned to keep his glances chaste.[2]

Fāris said: "The gnostic is the man whose knowledge is a spiritual condition, and whose motions are an overwhelming."[3] Junayd, being asked concerning the gnostic, said: "The colour of the water is the colour of the vessel." He meant, that in every state he follows what is more proper: now his states are diverse, and that is the reason why he is called "the son of his time." Dhu 'l-Nūn said in answer to the same enquiry: "He was here, and departed", meaning that the gnostic

[1] Sc. an affliction instead of a refreshment.

[2] As the beginner first learns to concentrate only on God, so the gnostic must do.

[3] Sc. he is controlled in all his actions by God.

is never seen on two occasions in the same state, because he is controlled by Another. The following verse is assigned to Ibn 'Aṭā:

If time had tongues to speak, they would relate
That in the robe of passion I delight:
But time knows not my true and high estate,
For I move ever to a loftier height.

Sahl ibn 'Abdillāh said: "The first station in gnosis is when the mystic is granted a certainty in his heart by which his members find repose, and a trustfulness in his members by which he is secure in this world, and a life in his soul by which he is victorious in his future state."

The gnostic, then, has made every effort to discharge his duty to God, and his gnosis is a realisation of what God has given him: therefore he truly returns from things to God. God says: "You will see their eyes gush with tears at what they recognise as truth."[1] Perhaps what is meant by "what they recognise" is what they have known of God's goodness and kindness, and His seeking them out and turning to them, and choosing them from among their fellows. So it was with Ubayy ibn Ka'b. The Prophet said to him: "Verily, God has commanded me to recite before thee." Ubayy said: "O Messenger of God! am I also mentioned here?" The Prophet said: "Yes."[2] So Ubayy wept: for he saw no state in which to face God, no gratitude to equal His bounties, no recollection worthy of Him; therefore he was silent, and wept. The Prophet also said to Ḥārithah: "Thou hast known, so cleave (to it)"; he related him to gnosis, and bade him cleave to that, not indicating for him any act. Dhu 'l-Nūn, being asked concerning the gnostic, said: "He is a man who, being with them, is yet apart from them." Sahl said: "They who have gnosis of God are like the

[1] S. v. 86.
[2] For this well-known Tradition, *vide* Wensinck, *Handbook*, pp. 232 f.

men of A'rāf, who 'know each by marks';[1] God has set them in their station, and raised them up above the two abodes, giving them knowledge of the two kingdoms." One of the Ṣūfīs wrote these lines:

Alas, for those who have completed
    This earthly course, and gone their way!
Long years with them have I competed:
    The part they played I cannot play.

Their lives were secret and secluded
    Midst all the pride of royal state;[2]
Men cried, who saw them thus denuded,
    "They are unformed, inanimate!"[3]

Chapter LXIII

THEIR DOCTRINE OF THE SEEKER AND THE SOUGHT

The seeker is in reality the sought, and the Sought the Seeker: for the man who seeks God only seeks Him because God first sought him. So God says, "He loves them, and they love Him";[4] and again, "God was well-pleased with them, and they were well-pleased with God";[5] and again, "Then He turned to them, that they might turn".[6] His seeking of them was the cause of their seeking Him: for the cause of every thing is God's act, and His act has no cause. If God seeks a man, it is not possible for that man not to seek God: so God has made the seeker the sought, and the Sought the Seeker. Nevertheless (in the language of the Ṣūfīs), the seeker is the man whose toiling preceded his revelation, while the sought is he whose revelation preceded

[1] S. vii. 44. A'rāf is the bridge over heaven and hell.
[2] The "beggars in silk and kings in rags" theme. Cf. *supra*, p. 2, n. 4.
[3] A quotation from the verses of Junayd cited on *supra*, p. 115.
[4] S. v. 59. [5] S. v. 119. [6] S. ix. 119.

his toiling. The seeker is described in God's words: "But those who fight strenuously for us we will surely guide them into our way."[1] Such a man is sought by God, Who turns his heart and implants in it a grace, to stir him to toil for Him, and to turn to Him, and to seek Him: then He accords him the revelation of the spiritual states. So it was with Ḥārithah, who said: "I turned myself from this world, and thirsted in the daytime, and watched at night"—then he said—"and it was as though I beheld the Throne of my Lord coming forth." With these words he indicated that the revelation of the unseen came to him after he had turned from this world. The "sought" man, on the other hand, is drawn forcibly out by God, and accorded the revelation of the states that through the power of vision he may be stirred to toil for God, and turn to Him, and bear the burdens laid on him by God. So it was with Pharaoh's magicians: after they had received the revelation, it was easy for them to endure the threats of Pharaoh, for they said, "We will never prefer thee to what has come to us of manifest signs.... Decide then what thou canst decide."[2] So it was with 'Umar ibn al-Khaṭṭāb, when he came seeking to slay the Prophet: for God waylaid him on his path.[3] Similar too is the story of Ibrāhīm ibn Adham:[4] he went out to hunt for pleasure, and a voice called him, saying, "Not for this wast thou created, and not to this wast thou commanded." Twice the voice called him; and on the third occasion the call came from the pommel of his saddle. Then he said: "By God, I will not disobey God henceforth, so long as my Lord protects me from sin." This, then, is what is meant by being

[1] S. xxix. 69. [2] S. xx. 75.

[3] For the story of his conversion, *vide* Ibn Hishām, pp. 224 ff.

[4] This well-known story is also related by Qushayrī, *Risālah* (Cairo, 1284), p. 10: the fullest biography of Ibrāhīm b. Adham is that given by Ibn 'Asākir, *Ta'rīkh Dimashq* (Damascus, 1330), II, pp. 167 ff.

"drawn forcibly": these men were granted revelation of spiritual states, and were thereby expelled from their carnal appetites and their possessions. The lawyer Abū 'Abdillāh al-Baraqī once quoted these verses to me, his own composition:

> The seeker's heart is based in purity,
> And passion leads his steps in every glen;
> Along whatever vale his course may be,
> His only refuge is the Lord of men.
>
> He paid with purity, and purely paid,
> And pureness to his heart a lantern brought.
> His seeking was upon the Seeker stayed:
> Thrice-blessed is the seeker who is sought!

Chapter LXIV

THEIR DOCTRINE OF TOILING AND DIVINE PRACTICE

One of the great Ṣūfīs said: "True service is the performance of what God has imposed as a duty, provided it be understood that it is an obligation, that is, that it must be accomplished with no consideration of compensation, even though thou knowest this to be a (divine) bounty: thy duty to God suffices, during the performance of the act, to drive out all consideration of bounty and compensation. For God says: 'Verily, God hath bought of the believers their persons and their wealth',[1] that is, that they may serve Him as slaves, not in the spirit of covetousness."

A man said to Abū Bakr al-Wāsiṭī: "With what motive must the mystic engage in his motions?" He replied: "With the motive of having passed away from his motions, which exist through another than he."[2] Abū 'Abdillāh al-Nibājī said: "Pleasure in obedience is the fruit of estrangement from God. A man is not

[1] S. ix. 112.

[2] That is, through God.

joined with God because of it, or severed (from God because of not possessing it): he does not trust to it as something to be relied on, nor does he leave it in the spirit of rebellion. He merely performs his duties to God as a slave and a servant, relying on what was (destined by God) in pre-eternity." By "pleasure in obedience" he means, supposing it to proceed from oneself, without seeing God's bounty in aiding one (to be obedient). The words of God, "Surely the mention of God is greater"[1] are interpreted as meaning, that they are greater than your understandings can attain, or your intellects contain, or your tongues express. True recollection consists in forgetting what is other than God, for God says: "And remember thy Lord when thou hast forgotten."[2] So the words of God, "Eat ye and drink with good digestion, for what ye did aforetime in the empty days"[3], are interpreted as meaning, empty of God's recollection, that ye may know that ye obtained what ye obtained through God's favour, not because of your own actions.

Abū Bakr al-Qaḥtabī said: "The souls of the unitarians are disgusted with all their attributes and qualities which have been manifested, and everything that has appeared from them they find abhorrent. They are cut off from their attestations, their acquirements and their advantages, and are unable to manifest any claim before Him, for they have heard Him say, 'and join none in the service of his Lord'."[4] By "attestations" he means mankind, by "advantages" compensations, and by "acquirements" material things. Abū Bakr al-Wāsiṭī said: "The meaning of the saying 'God is great' during prayer is as if one said, Thou art too mighty to be joined with by prayer, or to be separated from by omitting to pray: for separation and union are not (personal) motions, they follow a course preordained in eternity." Al-Junayd said: "Let not thy purpose in

[1] S. xxix. 44.
[2] S. xviii. 23.
[3] S. lxix. 24.
[4] S. xviii. 110.

thy prayer be, to perform it, without taking pleasure and joy in the union with Him to Whom there is no means of approach save through Himself." Ibn 'Aṭā said: "Let not thy purpose in thy prayer be, to perform it, without awe and reverence for Him Who has seen thee performing it." Another said: "The meaning of prayer is detachment from encumbrances, and separation with realities." Encumbrances are everything other than God, realities are the things which are for God and of God. Another said: "Prayer is a joining." I heard Fāris say: "The meaning of fasting is to be absent from the sight of men in the sight of God. For God says, in the story of Mary, 'Verily, I have vowed to the Merciful One a fast, and I will not speak today with a human being'[1]: that is, because I am absent from them in the vision of God, and therefore I cannot include in my fast anything that may distract or cut me off from Him." This is proved by the Prophet's saying, "Fasting is a preservation",[2] that is, a veil over everything but God. God also says, "Fasting is Mine, and I will reward for it": one of the great Ṣūfīs said, "That means, I am the reward for it." Abu 'l-Ḥasan ibn Abī Dharr said: "That means, my gnosis is his reward for it. Surely that is a sufficient reward, for there is nothing that can attain God's gnosis, or so much as come near it." I heard Abu 'l-Ḥasan al-Ḥasanī al-Hamadānī say: "The meaning of the saying, 'Fasting is Mine', is that the desires may leave it: that is, first the desire of the devil, lest he corrupt it, for the devil does not desire what is God's; secondly, the desire of the soul, lest it boast thereof, for it only boasts of what belongs to it; and thirdly, the desire of the adversaries in the world to come, for they only take what belongs to man, not what belongs to God." This is the meaning of God's saying, as far as I have been able to understand.

[1] S. xix. 27.

[2] For this and the following Tradition, *vide* Wensinck, *Handbook*, pp. 71 f.

A Ṣūfī said: "The trouble of the affliction is the regard for the appetites and the reliance that is put in the personal actions: if one trusts to them, the consequence is misery; and in the attainment of misery is the joy of one's enemies."[1] Al-Nūrī wrote:

"Today I wellnigh reach my goal!" I cried:
    Alas, the wellnigh goal is very far.
I do not fight, but fail; yet, to have tried
    And lost the battle, that itself is war.[2]

Now every hope is lost, but that Thy love
Will yet forgive, Thy bounteousness approve:
Else heav'n is barred; I must in exile rove.

Another wrote:

Grant that I cherish and remember Thee
        In hope of gain:
So yearn the children of inconstancy[3]
        For pleasures vain.

How, Lord, shall I Thy glorious revelation
        Aspire to bear,
And leave this world of veiling and temptation
        In transport rare?

He says: if in my actions and endeavours I look for Thy reward therefor—and this is what is sought by the people who labour and strive to godliness—how shall I consider the revelation of that which transports me from the fear of the issue of my changing states and moments, and from regarding my own motions and endeavours, which are the things that veil me from Thee?

[1] This is a commentary on the prayer ascribed to the Prophet: "O God! I take refuge with Thee from the trouble of the affliction, the attainment of misery, and the joy of the enemy."

[2] Sc. there is merit in having attempted, even if the attempt has failed.

[3] Sc. the children of this world.

Chapter LXV

THEIR DOCTRINE OF DISCOURSING TO MEN

A man said to Al-Nūrī: "When may a man presume to discourse to his fellows?" He replied: "When he understands concerning God, then it is right that he should make God's servants understand: but when he does not understand concerning God, then his affliction is common to all the land, and is over all men." Sarī al-Saqaṭī said: "I recall how men come to me, and I say, O God! grant them such knowledge as may keep them from me, for I do not like their coming to me." Sahl said: "For thirty years I was speaking to God, and men imagined that I was speaking to them." Al-Junayd said to Al-Shiblī: "We studied this science deeply, and then concealed it in the vaults: but thou hast come and displayed it above the heads of the people." Al-Shiblī replied: "I speak, and I listen: is there any other in the world but I?" One of the great Ṣūfīs said to Al-Junayd, when he was discoursing to the people: "O Abu 'l-Qāsim! God does not approve of him who possesses a certain knowledge, until He finds him living in that knowledge: so if thou art in the knowledge, remain where thou art, but if not, descend." So Al-Junayd arose, and did not discourse with men for two months. Then he came out, and said: "If it had not been that I have heard that the Prophet said, 'In the last days the champion of the people shall be the vilest among them', I would not have come forth to you." Al-Junayd also said: "I never discoursed to the people, until thirty of the most distinguished men had indicated me, saying, 'Thou art fit to call (others) to God'." A man asked one of the great mystics: "Why dost thou not discourse?" He replied: "This is a world that has turned its back and departed: and the man who goes after one who has turned his back is more backward than the other."[1] Abū Manṣūr al-Panjakhīnī said to Abu 'l-Qāsim al-Ḥakīm: "With what intention shall I discourse to the people?" He replied: "I know of no intention with regard to disobedience, other than to give it up." Abū 'Uthmān Sa'īd ibn Ismā'īl al-Rāzī asked Abū Ḥafṣ al-Ḥaddād, whose pupil he was, for permission to discourse publicly. Abū Ḥafṣ asked him: "And what prompts thee to do so?" He replied: "I pity them, and would counsel them." The other asked: "What is the measure of thy pity for them?" He answered: "If I knew that God would punish me instead of all those who believe in Him, and would bring them to Paradise, I would find my heart acquiescent therein." Abū Ḥafṣ thereupon granted him permission. Now he attended his first seance: and when Abū 'Uthmān had finished his discourse, a man stood up to beg. Abū 'Uthmān forestalled him by giving him the coat which he was wearing. Then Abū Ḥafṣ said: "Thou liar, beware of discoursing to men, so long as this thing[2] is in thee." Abū 'Uthmān asked: "What thing, master?" He replied: "Wouldst thou not so counsel them, and didst thou not so much pity them, as to prefer that they should have the reward of preceding thee, and that thou shouldst follow them?"[3] I heard the following narrative of Fāris, who had it from Abū 'Amr al-Anmāṭī: "We were with Al-Junayd, when Al-Nūrī passed by, and greeted him." Al-Junayd replied: "And on thee be peace, O commander of the hearts.[4] Speak!" Al-Nūrī said: "O Abu 'l-Qāsim! thou hast deceived them, and they have set thee in the pulpits; I have counselled them, and they have cast me on the dunghills." Al-Junayd said: "I have never known my heart more sorrowful than it was at that

[1] Sc. it is no use trying to teach the obstinate.

[2] Some MSS. read "this greed".

[3] Abū 'Uthmān is wrong to seek the merit of giving, which should belong to the beggar.

[4] A turn of the Caliph's title, Commander of the Faithful.

moment." The next Friday he came to us, and said: "When thou seest the Ṣūfī discoursing to men, know that he is empty." Ibn 'Aṭā said: "God's words, 'And speak to them words that may penetrate their souls',[1] mean, (speak to them) according to the capacity of their understandings and the limit of their intellects." Another said: "God's words, 'But if he had fabricated concerning us any sayings, we had surely seized him by the right hand',[2] mean, if he had spoken of ecstatic things of the people of material lives." This interpretation is confirmed by another saying: "Deliver to them what has been sent down to thee from thy Lord";[3] God did not say, "Deliver to them that whereby we have made ourselves known to thee." Al-Ḥusayn al-Maghāzilī saw Ruwaym ibn Muḥammad discoursing to the people on the subject of poverty; he stopped, and said to him:

> Why wearest thou this flashing blade,
> By which no man was ever flayed?
> Proud hero with thy sword so bold,
> Go, get an anklet wrought of gold![4]

He means to infer that he was describing a state in which he had never himself been. One of the great Ṣūfīs said: "If a man discourses without knowing the meaning of what he is discoursing upon, he is like an ass in his pretension. God says: 'Like an ass supporting a load of books'."[5]

Chapter LXVI

OF THEIR PIETY AND PIOUS ENDEAVOURS

Al-Ḥārith al-Muḥāsibī inherited from his father more than 30,000 dinars, but would not touch a penny of it,

[1] S. iv. 66. [2] S. lxix. 44. [3] S. v. 71.
[4] Sc. do not talk of things about which thou knowest nothing.
[5] S. lxii. 5.

saying: "He was a Qadarite."[1] Abū 'Uthmān said: "I was in the house of Abū Bakr ibn Abī Ḥanīfah with Abū Ḥafṣ. We happened to mention an absent friend, and Abū Ḥafṣ said, 'If I had a sheet of paper, I would write to him.' I said, 'Here is a sheet.' Now Abū Bakr had gone out to the market. Abū Ḥafṣ replied, 'Perhaps Abū Bakr has died, without our knowing it, and the sheet has become the property of his heirs.' He therefore abstained from writing." Abū 'Uthmān also said: "I was with Abū Ḥafṣ, when he had a quantity of raisins. I took one raisin, and put it in my mouth. He immediately seized me by the throat, and said, 'Thou cheat, thou art eating my raisin.' I replied, 'I was confident of your abstinence in the matters of this world, for I knew that you were unselfish, and for this reason I took the raisin.' He answered, 'O foolish man! thou trustest a heart which is not ruled by its master'." I heard many of our Shaykhs say: "The Shaykhs would abstain from intercourse with a poor man for one of three reasons: if he performed the pilgrimage having accepted money from another; if he went to Khurāsān; and if he entered Yemen. They said: 'If he comes to Khurāsān, he only does so in order to obtain ease, and in Khurāsān there is nothing lawful or good to eat; and as for Yemen, there are many ways there to corruption'." Abu 'l-Mughīth would never rest or sleep on his side, but all night remained in prayer standing: and whenever his eyes grew weary,[2] he would sit down and place his forehead on his knees, and doze a little. A man said to him: "Be kind to thyself."[3] He replied: "The Kindly God has not been kind to me, that I should have ease of it. Hast thou not heard that the Lord of the Emissaries said, 'The most afflicted of men are the prophets, then the true believers, then the like and the like'." It is said that

[1] And therefore, according to the stricter view, a heretic, so that his property was not fit for a Muslim to inherit.

[2] Lit. "overcame him".

[3] Sc. give thyself a little ease.

Abū 'Amr al-Zajjājī dwelt at Mecca many years, and never performed a natural need in the Sacred Territory, but always went outside to do so, and then returned in a condition of ritual purity. I heard Fāris tell the following anecdote: "Abū 'Abdillāh known as Shikthal[1] would not speak with men, but took refuge in deserts which are in the district of Kūfah, eating nothing but permitted food and sweepings. I met him one day, and attaching myself to him said: 'I ask thee in God's name, wilt thou not tell me what it is that prevents thee from discoursing?' He replied: 'O man! this existence is but a fancy in the midst of reality, and it is not right to speak of a thing which possesses no reality. And as for the Real, words fail to describe Him: so where is the use of discoursing?' And he left me, and passed on his way." Fāris also told me that he heard Al-Ḥusayn al-Maghāzilī say: "I saw 'Abdullāh al-Qashshā' one night standing on the bank of the Tigris, and saying, 'My Lord, I thirst; my Lord, I thirst!' So he continued until morning; then he said: 'Alas! Thou makest a thing lawful to me, and preventest me from taking it; and Thou makest a thing unlawful to me, and givest me free access to it: what then shall I do?' So he returned, and did not drink." I heard the same person also relate that he heard a certain poor man say: "In the year of the Plain[2] I was in the company of certain men: I left them, and later returned and went around among the wounded. I saw Abū Muḥammad al-Jurayrī, who was then more than a hundred years old, and said to him: 'Sir, why dost thou not pray, that this (calamity) which thou seest may be removed?' He replied: 'I have done so.' And he added: 'Verily, I do whatsoever I will.'[3] I repeated my request to him, and

[1] Other MSS. read: Shiksal, Saksal, Sakīl.

[2] The commentator identifies this with the year 315, the first year in which the Carmathians waylaid the pilgrimage. *Vide* Muir, *The Caliphate* (3rd ed.), p. 564.

[3] Sc. as God says of Himself.

he said: 'My brother, this is not the time for prayer, this is the time for acquiescence and resignation.' I said to him: 'Dost thou need aught?' He answered: 'I thirst.' So I brought him water, and he took it, and wished to drink it; then he looked at me, and said: 'These men thirst, and I drink. No, this is greed.' So he returned the water to me, and immediately he died." Fāris also related that he heard one of the companions of Al-Jurayrī say: "I remained for twenty years without the thought of food coming into my mind until it was brought to me; and I remained twenty years praying the prayer of dawn while still pure from the second evening prayer; and I remained for twenty years not making any compact with God, for fear lest He should prove me false out of my own mouth. I remained for twenty years, my tongue only listening to my heart; then my state changed, and I remained for twenty years, my heart only listening to my tongue." The meaning of his saying, "my tongue only listening to my heart", is, "I only spoke because of a reality which I possessed"; and of "my heart only listening to my tongue", "God preserved my tongue, as the Tradition says, 'By Me he hears, and by Me he sees, and by Me he speaks'."[1] One of our Shaykhs told me that he heard Muḥammad ibn Sa'dān say: "I served Abu 'l-Mughīth for twenty years, and never once saw him regret anything he had lost, or seek anything he had missed." It is said that Abu 'l-Sawdā performed the lesser pilgrimage sixty times, and Ja'far ibn Muḥammad al-Khuldī, fifty times. One of our Shaykhs—I am more inclined to think that it was Abū Ḥamzah al-Khurāsānī—performed the pilgrimage ten times for the sake of the Prophet, ten times for the ten companions of the Prophet,[2] and one pilgrimage on his own account: and he hoped by means of the other pilgrimages to win God's acceptance of his own pilgrimage.

[1] Cf. *supra* p. 138, n. 1.
[2] *Vide supra* p. 62, n. 1.

Chapter LXVII

OF GOD'S FAVOURS TO THE ṢŪFĪS AND HIS WARNING THEM BY MEANS OF SUPERNATURAL VOICES

Abū Sa'īd al-Kharrāz said: "On the evening of 'Arafah[1] the sense of God's nearness cut me off from the desire to petition God. Then my soul contended with me, that I should petition God; and I heard a voice saying: 'After thou hast found God, dost thou petition another than God?'" Abū Ḥamzah al-Khurāsānī said: "One year, when I performed the pilgrimage, I was walking along the road when I fell into a well. My soul contended with me that I should cry for help; but I said: 'No, by God, I will not cry out!' I had hardly completed this cogitation, when two men passed by at the top of the well, and one of them said to the other: 'Come, let us fill in the top of this well from the roadway.' So they brought a stick and a reed mat. I was moved to cry out; then I said: 'O Thou Who art nearer to me than they!' and I held my peace until they had filled in the well and gone away. Then I saw something dangling its feet into the well, and saying, 'Catch hold of me.' So I caught hold of it, and behold, it was a lion: and I heard a voice saying, 'O Abū Ḥamzah, this is excellent! We have rescued thee from destruction in the well by means of a lion'." One of our companions told me that he heard Abū Walīd relate the following story: "One day our companions brought me some milk, and I said, 'That will harm me.' Then one day I prayed to God, saying: 'O God, forgive me, for Thou knowest that I have never joined other gods with Thee even for the twinkling of an eye!' I heard a voice saying: 'Not even the night of

[1] Dhu 'l-Ḥijjah 9, on which the pilgrims halt at 'Arafah.

the milk?'"[1] Abū Sa'īd al-Kharrāz said: "Once I was in the desert, and was seized with a violent hunger. My soul demanded of me that I should ask God for food; and I said: 'That is not the act of one who puts his trust in God.' Then my soul demanded of me that I should petition God for patience; and as I was about to do this, I heard a voice saying:

'Lo, I am nigh!' he shouts in pride:
 But never man who came
To seek our succour was denied,
 And sent away in shame.

So feebly cries the man of might
 In weakness dolorous,
As if we never were in sight
 Of him, nor he of us."

That the phenomenon of the supernatural voice is genuine is attested by the following story:[2] When they wished to wash the (body of the) Prophet, they were divided on the matter, saying: "By God, we know not whether we should strip the Prophet of his clothes, as we do with our dead, or wash him with his clothes still on him." As they were thus divided, God put them into a slumber, until every one of them had his chin resting on his chest. Then a voice addressed them from the direction of the Kaaba—and none knew whose it was—and said: "Wash the Prophet with his clothes still upon him."[3]

[1] Sc. in saying, "that will harm me", when only God has the power to harm or profit.

[2] The following *isnād* is quoted: Muḥammad b. Muḥammad b. Maḥmūd > Naṣr b. Zakariyyā > 'Ammār b. al-Ḥasan > Salamah b. al-Faḍl > Muḥammad b. Isḥāq > Yaḥyā b. 'Abbād b. 'Abdillāh b. al-Zubayr > 'Abbād b. 'Abdillāh > 'Ā'ishah.

[3] Cf. Ibn Hishām, pp. 1018 f.

Chapter LXVIII

OF GOD'S WARNING THEM BY GIFTS OF INSIGHT

Abu 'l-'Abbās ibn al-Muhtadī said: "I was once in the desert, and I saw a man walking before me with feet bare and head uncovered, and he was carrying no wallet. I said to myself: 'How can this man pray? He has neither purity nor prayer.' Thereupon he turned to me, and said: 'He knows what is in your souls, wherefore fear Him.'[1] Immediately I fainted: and when I recovered, I asked God's pardon for the regard which I had cast upon him. Then, as I was walking along the road, he came again before me: and as I looked at him, I feared him, and stopped. But he turned to me, and recited: 'It is He that accepts the repentance of His servants, and pardons their evil-doings.'[2] Then he disappeared, and I never saw him again."[3] Abu 'l-Ḥasan al-Fārisī told me that he heard Abu 'l-Ḥasan al-Muzayyin say: "I went into the desert alone, to be apart from men. When I was at Al-'Umaq,[4] I sat down on the margin of the pool there, and my soul began to speak to me about how it had gone apart from men, and journeyed through the desert, and a sense of pride entered into it. Then, behold, Al-Kattānī appeared to me"—or it may have been another, the doubt is mine—"on the other side of the pool, and called me, saying: 'O cupper! how long wilt thou speak to thyself of vain things?'"—It is also related that the voice said: "O cupper! do not speak to thyself of vain things." Dhu 'l-Nūn said: "I once saw a youth wearing old rags, and my soul revolted against him, yet my heart attested that he was a saint. So I remained

1 S. ii. 236. 2 S. xlii. 24.
3 Kalābādhī adds: "or whatever he said".
4 A station on the road to Mecca.

divided between my soul and my heart, reflecting. The youth perceived what was in my mind, for looking towards me he said: 'O D͟hu 'l-Nūn, do not look at me in order to see what is my character. The pearl is only to be found within the shell.' Then he turned away, reciting:

I hold the world in proud neglect,
    My kingdom no man shares:
I am a youth of intellect,
    I know my worth and theirs.

I am a ruler and a king,
    Let fortune smile or frown,
For freedom is my covering,
    Contentment is my gown."

That spiritual insight is a genuine phenomenon is attested by the following Tradition:[1] "Fear the insight of the believer, for verily he sees with the light of God."

Chapter LXIX

OF GOD'S WARNING THEM BY MEANS OF THOUGHTS

Abū Bakr ibn Mujāhid al-Muqrī' related the following story. Abū 'Amr ibn al-'Alā came forward one day to lead the congregation in prayer. Now he was not an Imām, that he should be required to come forward. Having stepped out, he said to the people: "Settle yourselves." Then he fainted, and did not recover until the following day. When questioned about this afterwards, he said: "At the moment when I said to you, 'Settle yourselves', a thought from God came into my heart, as if God were saying to me, 'O my servant!

[1] The following is the *isnād*: Aḥmad b. 'Alī > T͟hawāb b. Yazīd al-Mawṣilī > Ibrāhīm b. al-Hayt͟ham al-Baladī > Abū Ṣāliḥ Kātib al-Layt͟h > Mu'āwiyah b. Ṣāliḥ > Rās͟hid b. Sa'īd > Abū Umāmah al-Bāhilī.

hast thou settled thyself with Me for but the twinkling of an eye, that thou shouldst command others to settle themselves?'" Al-Junayd said: "Once I was sick, and prayed to God that He might heal me. He said to me in my conscience: 'Enter not between Me and thy soul'."[1] One of our companions heard Muḥammad ibn Sa'dān relate that he heard one of the great Ṣūfīs say: "Whenever I doze awhile, I hear a voice calling me, and saying, 'Sleepest thou to Me? If thou sleepest to Me, verily, I will strike thee with a whip'."

Chapter LXX

OF GOD'S WARNING THEM THROUGH VISIONS AND RARE FAVOURS

Abū Bakr Muḥammad ibn Ghālib told me that he was informed by Muḥammad ibn Khafīf that he heard Abū Bakr Muḥammad ibn 'Alī al-Kattānī say: "I saw the Prophet as I was wont to do"—now it was his wont to see the Prophet every Monday and Thursday night, when he would ask him questions, which the Prophet would answer—"and I saw him coming towards me with four persons. Then he said to me: 'O Abū Bakr! knowest thou who this is?' I answered: 'Yes, it is Abū Bakr.' He asked: 'Knowest thou this man?' I answered: 'Yes, he is 'Umar.' He asked: 'Knowest thou this man?' I answered: 'Yes, he is 'Uthmān.' He said: 'Knowest thou this fourth person?' Thereat I hesitated, and did not answer. The Prophet repeated the question, and I still hesitated; he asked it a third time, and again I hesitated: for I was jealous for him. Then the Prophet clenched his hand, and pointed with it to me; then he spread it out, and struck me on the chest, saying: 'Say, O Abū Bakr! This is 'Alī ibn Abī

[1] For a man's soul belongs to God.

Ṭālib.' So I said: 'O Messenger of God! this is 'Alī ibn Abī Ṭālib.' The Prophet then introduced me to Alī, who put my hand in his, and said to me: 'Rise, Abū Bakr, and go forth unto Al-Ṣafā.'[1] And I went forth with him unto Al-Ṣafā, while I was yet sleeping in my room: and I awoke, and lo, I was at Al-Ṣafā."

Manṣūr ibn 'Abdillāh told me that he heard Abū 'Abdillāh ibn al-Jallā say: "I entered the city of the Prophet of God being somewhat in need. I went to the (Prophet's) grave, and saluted the Prophet and his two comrades, Abū Bakr and 'Umar; then I said: 'O Prophet of God! I have a need, and I am thy guest this night.' Then I turned aside, and slept between the grave and the pulpit: and lo, the Prophet came to me, and handed me a loaf. I ate half, and then awoke, and found in my hand half a loaf." Yūsuf ibn al-Ḥusayn said: "We had with us a youthful pupil, who had gone on to study the Ḥadīth before he had finished the reading of the Qur'ān. One came to him in sleep, and said to him:

> If thou hast not been so unkind
> To me, then why my book hast thou disdained?
> Consider, if thou be not blind,
> My subtle words which are therein contained."[2]

That visions are a genuine phenomenon is testified by the following narrative told by Al-Ḥasan al-Baṣrī:[3] "I entered the mosque of Baṣrah, and found a number of our companions seated there. I sat down with them, and heard them discussing a certain man, and scandalising him. I forbade them to discuss him, telling them various Traditions relating to the subject of backbiting which I had heard attributed to the Prophet and Jesus

[1] A place in Mecca.

[2] These lines, which in my text are printed as prose, can be read as verse, if the reading of Q.V. is adopted.

[3] The following *isnād* is quoted: 'Alī b. al-Ḥasan b. Aḥmad Imām of the mosque of Sarakhs > Abu 'l-Walīd Muḥammad b. Idrīs al-Sulamī > Suwayd > Muḥammad b. 'Amr b. Ṣāliḥ b. Mas'ūd al-Kilā'ī.

son of Mary. The people then refrained, and began to talk of another matter: but presently the name of this man came up again, and they discussed him in turn, and I with them. So they departed to their dwellings, and I to mine. As I slept, a black man came to me in my dream, carrying in his hand a wicker dish on which was a piece of swine's flesh. He said to me, 'Eat.' I said, 'I will not eat, this is swine's flesh.' He said, 'Eat.' I said, 'I will not eat, this is swine's flesh.' He said, 'Eat.' I said, 'I will not eat, this is swine's flesh, this is unlawful.' He said, 'Thou certainly shalt eat it.' Again I refused him. Then he opened my jaws, and put the meat in my mouth, and I began to chew it, while he continued to stand before me: I was afraid to cast it out, and at the same time I would not swallow it. In this state I awoke: and for thirty days and thirty nights thereafter nothing that I ate or drank gave me any pleasure, for I tasted in my mouth the savour of that flesh, and smelt its odour in my nostrils."

Chapter LXXI

GOD'S FAVOURS TO THEM WHICH SPRING OF HIS JEALOUSY

A number of persons came to visit Rābiʿah when she was suffering from a malady. They said to her: "What is thy state?" She replied: "By God, I know of no reason for my illness, except[1] that Paradise was displayed to me, and I yearned after it in my heart; and I think that my Lord was jealous for me, and so reproached me: and only He can make me happy."[2] Al-Junayd said: "I came to Sarī al-Saqaṭī, and found

[1] Following Q.V.

[2] Lit. "His is the power to leave off being angry with me", *vide* Lane, s.v.

a piece of broken pottery in his room. I said to him, 'What is this?' He replied: 'The day before yesterday, my little girl brought me a jar with water in it, and said to me, Father, this jar is hung up here: when it is cold, drink it, for it is a stifling night. When I fell asleep,[1] I saw a beautiful maid enter my room, and I said, Whose art thou? She replied, His who does not drink cold water in jars. Then she struck the jar with her hand, and it broke: and this is the jar thou seest.' The jar continued in the same place, without being moved, until it was covered with dust."

Al-Muzayyin said: "I once stayed in a desert-station for seven days, without anything passing my lips. Then a man invited me to his house, and offered me dates and bread: but I was unable to eat. When it was night, I felt a desire to eat, so I took a date-stone, and essayed to open my mouth with it. The stone broke my teeth. One of the girls of the house cried: 'Father, how much is our guest eating tonight?' I retorted: 'My master, a hunger seven days old, and then thou grudgest me. Nay, by Thy might, I will not taste it'."

Aḥmad ibn al-Samīn said: "I was once walking along the road to Mecca, when I heard a man crying out, 'O man of God, of God!' I said, 'What ails thee, what ails thee?' He replied, 'Take from me these dirhams: I cannot recollect God, so long as they are with me.' So I took them from him: and he cried out, 'God, here am I, here am I!' Now they were in number fourteen dirhams." Abu 'l-Khayr al-Aqṭa' was once asked what was the cause of his hand being cut off. He said: "I was in the mountains of Lukkām, or it may have been Lebanon, I and a friend of mine. There came a man from one of the governors, distributing dīnārs. He handed me one dīnār, and I stretched out the back of my hand, and he placed the dīnār on it; then I dropped the dīnār into my companion's lap, and stood up. An hour afterwards the governor's officers

[1] Lit. "when my eye overcame me".

came looking for thieves; and they took me, and cut off my hand."

The genuineness of this phenomenon is attested by the Tradition of the Prophet:[1] "God protects His servant from this world, when he loves Him, even as ye protect your sick."

Chapter LXXII

GOD'S BOUNTIES IN LAYING HARDSHIPS UPON THEM TO BEAR

Fāris told me that he heard Abu 'l-Ḥasan al-'Alawī, the pupil of Ibrāhīm al-Khawwāṣ, say: "I saw Al-Khawwāṣ in the mosque at Dīnawar, seated in the centre of it, while the snow was falling on him. I felt moved with compassion towards him, and said to him, 'What if thou shouldst move to shelter?' He replied, 'No.' Then he began to recite:

> The way to Thee is clear and wide,
> For none who seeks Thee needs a guide.
> In winter's cold Thou art my spring,
> In summer's heat, my covering.

Then he said to me: 'Give me thy hand.' I gave him my hand, and he placed it inside his gown, and behold, he was streaming with sweat." I heard Abu 'l-Ḥasan al-Fārisī say: "I was in a certain desert,[2] when I was affected by a violent thirst, so that I was unable through weakness to walk. Now I had heard that before a man dies of thirst, his eyes water: I therefore sat down, waiting for my eyes to water. Suddenly I heard a sound, and looking round I saw a white snake, shining

[1] The *isnād* is: Aḥmad b. Ḥayyān al-Tamīmī > Abū Isḥāq Ibrāhīm b. Ismā'īl > Qutaybah b. Sa'īd > Ya'qūb b. 'Abd al-Raḥmān al-Iskandarānī > 'Amr b. Abī 'Amr > 'Āṣim b. 'Umar b. Qutādah > Maḥmūd b. Labīd.

[2] Reading *bawādī* for *wādī*, which is a misprint.

like pure silver, and making rapidly for me. I was alarmed, and started up[1] in my fright, which put strength into me. In spite of my weakness I began to walk, while the snake was hissing behind me. I went on walking, until I came to water: then the sound ceased. I turned round, and could not see the snake: I drank the water, and was saved. Now, whenever I am afflicted with grief or sickness, as soon as I see this snake in my sleep, I recognise it as a sign that my grief is overcome and my sickness at an end."

Chapter LXXIII

GOD'S GRACE TO THEM AT DEATH AND AFTER

Abu 'l-Ḥasan, called Qazzāz, said: "We were at Al-Fajj,[2] when a handsome young man came to us, wearing two worn woollen garments. He saluted us, and said, 'Is there a clean place here where I may die?' We were much astonished, but replied that there was, and showed him the way to a well nearby. He went away, and performed his ablutions, and prayed awhile.[3] We waited an hour for him, and when he did not return, we came to him, and found that he was dead." The companions of Sahl ibn 'Abdillāh relate that when Sahl was being washed on the bier, he held the forefinger of his right hand erect and pointed with it. Abū 'Amr al-Iṣṭakhrī said: "I saw Abū Turāb al-Nakhshabī in the desert, standing up, dead, and with nothing supporting him." Ibrāhīm ibn Shaybān said:

[1] The MSS. vary: some read "so I screamed out", others "so I continued".

[2] Most probably this is the name of a place, though it may of course mean "in the pass".

[3] Lit. "as much as God willed".

"A disciple came to my house, and was sick there some days, and then died. After he had been put into his grave, I wished to uncover his cheek, and place it in the dust as a sign of humility, that haply God might have mercy on him. He smiled in my face, and said to me: 'Thou humblest me before Him Who dallies with me?' I replied: 'No, my friend. Is there life after death?' He answered: 'Knowest thou not that His friends do not die, but are moved from one abode to another?'" Ibrāhīm ibn Shaybān also said: "I knew a young man in my village who was pious, and never left the mosque, and I was very devoted to him. One day he fell sick. On a Friday I went to the town to pray: and it was my custom, whenever I went to town, to spend the rest of the day and night with my brothers. After the noon I felt disquieted, and so I returned to the village when dusk had fallen. I enquired after the youth, and they said, 'We think that he is in pain.' I went to him, and greeted him, and shook hands with him: and as we shook hands, his spirit departed. I then proceeded to wash him, and by mistake poured water on his left hand instead of his right: his hand was withdrawn from mine, and the lote-leaves which were on it fell off. Those who were with me fainted. He opened his eyes and looked at me, and I was startled, and prayed over him. Then I entered the grave to cover him: and when I unveiled his face, he opened his eyes and smiled, until his back-teeth and incisors showed. So we made the earth even over him, and scattered dust upon him."

That this phenomenon is genuine is attested by the following story.[1] Al-Rabī' ibn Khirāsh had sworn that he would not laugh again, until he knew whether he was in Paradise or hell. So he continued, and no man

[1] The following *isnād* is quoted: Abu 'l-Ḥasan 'Alī b. Ismā'īl al-Fārisī > Naṣr b. Aḥmad al-Baghdādī > Al-Walīd b. Shujā' al-Sakūnī > Khālid > Nāfi' al-Ash'arī > Ḥafṣ b. Yazīd b. Mas'ūd b. Khirāsh.

saw him laugh, until he died.[1] They closed his eyes, and covered him: then they ordered his grave to be dug, and his winding-sheet to be brought. Rab'ī his brother said: "My brother of us all kept most vigil during the long night, and fasted most during the hot day." As they were seated around him, the clothes were removed from his face, and he greeted them with a smile. His brother Rab'ī said: "My brother, is there life after death?" He replied: "Yes. I have met my Lord, and He received me with ease and repose, and a Lord Who is not angry. He has clothed me with brocade and silk, and I have found the matter to be easier than ye suppose: so do not be deceived. And now my friend Muḥammad awaits me, to pray for me:[2] hasten therefore, hasten!" Then, as he finished, his breath departed, like (the sound of) pebbles thrown into water. This story was told to 'Ā'ishah, the mother of the faithful; and she said: "A brother of the sons of 'Abs,[3] may God have mercy on his soul. I heard the Prophet say: 'A man shall speak after he is dead, of my community, one of the best of the Followers'."

Chapter LXXIV

OF OTHER GRACES ACCORDED THEM

Abū Bakr al-Qaḥṭabī said: "I was at the meeting of Sumnūn, when a man stood up and asked him concerning love. He said: 'I know of nobody today whom I am at liberty to address on this subject, and who would understand it.' At that moment a bird alighted on his head, and fell on his knee, saying, 'If there were

[1] The author adds "apparently".
[2] Or, "that prayer may be said for me".
[3] A tribe of the Arabs, who supported the Anti-Prophet Ṭulayḥah.

any, it would be this.'[1] So he began to say, pointing to the bird: 'I have heard such and such of the states of the people, and they experienced such and such, and were in such and such a spiritual condition.' So he continued to address the bird, until it fell from his knee, dead."

Abū Bakr ibn Mujāhid relates that Aḥmad ibn Sinān al-'Aṭṭār said that he heard one of his companions say: "One day I went out to Wāsiṭ, and saw a white bird in the midst of the water, saying: 'God is glorified above the forgetfulness of men'." Al-Junayd said: "I met a young disciple sitting in the desert under a tree, and I said to him: 'Young man, why sittest thou here?' He replied: 'I seek that which is lost.' I went away and left him: and when I had gone a little way, again I saw him, for he had been removed to a spot near me. I said to him: 'Why sittest thou here now?' He replied: 'I have found that for which I was searching in this spot, and so I have kept to it.' And I do not know which of that man's two states was the nobler: his application in seeking his state, or his persistence in keeping to the spot where he attained his desire."

Abū 'Abdillāh Muḥammad ibn Sa'dān relates that he heard one of the great Ṣūfīs say: "One day I was sitting opposite the Kaaba, when I heard a wailing noise proceeding from the building, and the words: 'O wall, move out of the way of my saints and friends: for whoso visits thee, processes about thee, but whoso visits Me, processes in My presence'."

[1] Sc. the bird: these words may have been said by Sumnūn himself.

Chapter LXXV

OF AUDITION

Audition is a resting after the fatigue of the (spiritual) moment, and a recreation for those who experience (spiritual) states, as well as a means of awakening the consciences of those who busy themselves with other things. It is preferred to other means of resting the natural qualities, because the soul is unlikely to cling to it or repose in it: for it comes and goes according to God's decree. Those mystics who enjoy revelation and direct experience have no need of such helps, for they have means which transport their hearts to walk[1] in the gardens of revelation.

I heard Fāris say: "I was with Qūṭah al-Mawṣilī, who had remained for forty years near a column in the mosque at Baghdad. We said to him: 'Here is an excellent singer. Shall we call him to thee?' He replied: 'My case is too grievous for any person to release me, or for any words to penetrate me. I am entirely impervious'."

When audition strikes the ears, it stirs the secret things of the heart: and a man is then either confused, because he is too weak to support the visitation, or his spiritual state gives him the power to control himself. Abū Muḥammad Ruwaym said: "The people heard their first *dhikr*[2] when God addressed them, saying, 'Am I not your Lord?'[3] This *dhikr* was secreted in their hearts, even as the fact (thus communicated) was secreted in their intellects. So, when they heard the (Ṣūfī) *dhikr*, the secret things of their hearts appeared,

[1] This is the post-Classical, and condemned, meaning of the word *tanazzah*.

[2] Sc. "recollection of God", the Ṣūfī exercise of inducing ecstasy.

[3] S. vii. 181. This was at the creation.

and they were ravished, even as the secret things of their intellects appeared when God informed them of this,[1] and they believed."

I heard Abu 'l-Qāsim al-Baghdādī say: "Audition is of two kinds. One class of man listens to discourse, and derives therefrom an admonition: such a man only listens discriminately and with his heart[2] present. The other class listens to music,[3] which is the food of the spirit: and when the spirit obtains its food, it attains its proper station, and turns aside from the government of the body; and then there appears in the listener a commotion and a movement."

Abū 'Abdillāh al-Nibājī said: "Audition stirs thought and produces admonition: all else is a temptation." Al-Junayd said: "The mercy (of God) descends upon the poor man on three occasions: when he is eating, for he only eats when he is in need to do so; when he speaks, for he only speaks when he is compelled; and during audition, for he only listens in a state of ecstasy."

[1] Sc. through the revelation of the Qur'ān, which awoke the remembrance of what had taken place at creation.

[2] As the seat of the intellect.

[3] Lit. "melody".

INDEX

1. NAMES OF PERSONS AND PLACES

(*Abbreviations*: A. = Aḥmad. a. = abū. ʻA. = ʻAbd. ʻAA. = ʻAbdullāh. b. = ibn. Ḥa. = Ḥasan. Ḥu. = Ḥusayn. M. = Muḥammad. The article *al-* is omitted.)

2. TECHNICAL TERMS